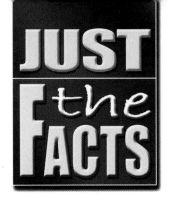

JUST the FACTS

INVENTIONS & DISCOVERIES

School Specialty
Publishing

Columbus, Ohio

This edition published in the United States in 2006 by School Specialty Publishing, a member of the School Specialty Family.
Copyright © ticktock Entertainment Ltd 2005 First published in Great Britain in 2005 by ticktock Media Ltd. Printed in China.

Written by Dee Phillips, Brian Alchorn, Catherine Chambers, David Dalton, Dougal Dixon, Ian Graham, Colin Hynson, Clint Twist, and Richard Walker. We would like to thank: Wendy and David Clemson, Evelyn Alchorn, Steve Owen, and Elizabeth Wiggans.
Library of Congress-in-Publication Data is on file with the publisher.

Send all inquiries to:
School Specialty Publishing
8720 Orion Place
Columbus, OH 43240-2111

ISBN 0-7696- 4256-X
1 2 3 4 5 6 7 8 9 10 TTM 11 10 09 08 07 06

CONTENTS

HOW TO USE THIS BOOK

JUST THE FACTS, INVENTIONS AND DISCOVERIES is a quick and easy-to-use way to look up facts about inventions, inventors, and famous discoveries. Every page is packed with names, places, dates, and key pieces of information. For fast access to just the facts, follow the tips on these pages.

BOX HEADINGS
Look for heading words linked to your research to guide you to the right fact box

INTRODUCTION TO TOPIC

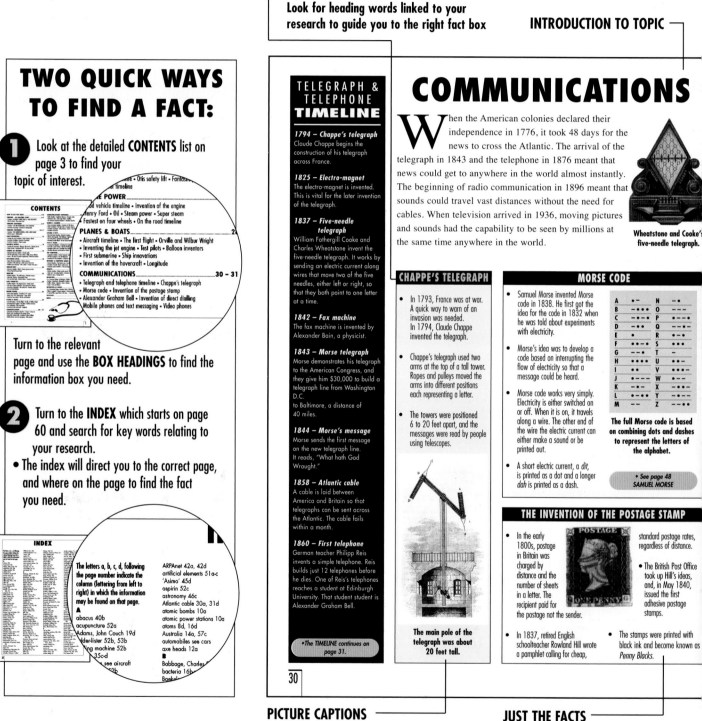

TWO QUICK WAYS TO FIND A FACT:

1 Look at the detailed **CONTENTS** list on page 3 to find your topic of interest.

Turn to the relevant page and use the **BOX HEADINGS** to find the information box you need.

2 Turn to the **INDEX** which starts on page 60 and search for key words relating to your research.
• The index will direct you to the correct page, and where on the page to find the fact you need.

CONTENTS (partial, in illustration)

... • Otis safety lift • Fantas... timeline

E POWER
...d vehicle timeline • Invention of the engine
...Henry Ford • Oil • Steam power • Super steam
• Fastest on four wheels • On the road timeline

PLANES & BOATS ... 2
• Aircraft timeline • The first flight • Orville and Wilbur Wright
• Inventing the jet engine • Test pilots • Balloon inventors
• First submarine • Ship innovations
• Invention of the hovercraft • Longitude

COMMUNICATIONS ... 30 – 31
• Telegraph and telephone timeline • Chappe's telegraph
• Morse code • Invention of the postage stamp
• Alexander Graham Bell • Invention of direct dialling
• Mobile phones and text messaging • Video phones

INDEX (partial, in illustration)

The letters a, b, c, d, following the page number indicate the column (lettering from left to right) in which the information may be found on that page.

A
abacus 40b
acupuncture 52a
...dder-lister 52b, 53b
...ng machine 52b
...35cd
... see aircraft
...2b

ARPAnet 42a, 42d
artificial elements 51a-c
'Asimo' 45d
aspirin 52c
astronomy 46c
Atlantic cable 30a, 31d
atomic bombs 10a
atomic power stations 10a
atoms 8d, 16d
Australia 14a, 57c
automobiles see cars
axe heads 12a
B
Babbage, Charles...
bacteria 16b
Bank...

TELEGRAPH & TELEPHONE TIMELINE

1794 – Chappe's telegraph
Claude Chappe begins the construction of his telegraph across France.

1825 – Electro-magnet
The electro-magnet is invented. This is vital for the later invention of the telegraph.

1837 – Five-needle telegraph
William Fothergill Cooke and Charles Wheatstone invent the five-needle telegraph. It works by sending an electric current along wires that move two of the five needles, either left or right, so that they both point to one letter at a time.

1842 – Fax machine
The fax machine is invented by Alexander Bain, a physicist.

1843 – Morse telegraph
Morse demonstrates his telegraph to the American Congress, and they give him $30,000 to build a telegraph line from Washington D.C. to Baltimore, a distance of 40 miles.

1844 – Morse's message
Morse sends the first message on the new telegraph line. It reads, "What hath God Wrought."

1858 – Atlantic cable
A cable is laid between America and Britain so that telegraphs can be sent across the Atlantic. The cable fails within a month.

1860 – First telephone
German teacher Philipp Reis invents a simple telephone. Reis builds just 12 telephones before he dies. One of Reis's telephones reaches a student at Edinburgh University. That student student is Alexander Graham Bell.

• *The TIMELINE continues on page 31.*

30

COMMUNICATIONS

When the American colonies declared their independence in 1776, it took 48 days for the news to cross the Atlantic. The arrival of the telegraph in 1843 and the telephone in 1876 meant that news could get to anywhere in the world almost instantly. The beginning of radio communication in 1896 meant that sounds could travel vast distances without the need for cables. When television arrived in 1936, moving pictures and sounds had the capability to be seen by millions at the same time anywhere in the world.

Wheatstone and Cooke's five-needle telegraph.

CHAPPE'S TELEGRAPH

• In 1793, France was at war. A quick way to warn of an invasion was needed. In 1794, Claude Chappe invented the telegraph.

• Chappe's telegraph used two arms at the top of a tall tower. Ropes and pulleys moved the arms into different positions each representing a letter.

• The towers were positioned 6 to 20 feet apart, and the messages were read by people using telescopes.

The main pole of the telegraph was about 20 feet tall.

MORSE CODE

• Samuel Morse invented Morse code in 1838. He first got the idea for the code in 1832 when he was told about experiments with electricity.

• Morse's idea was to develop a code based on interrupting the flow of electricity so that a message could be heard.

• Morse code works very simply. Electricity is either switched on or off. When it is on, it travels along a wire. The other end of the wire the electric current can either make a sound or be printed out.

• A short electric current, a *dit*, is printed as a dot and a longer *dah* is printed as a dash.

A	• —	N	— •
B	— • • •	O	— — —
C	— • — •	P	• — — •
D	— • •	Q	— — • —
E	•	R	• — •
F	• • — •	S	• • •
G	— — •	T	—
H	• • • •	U	• • —
I	• •	V	• • • —
J	• — — —	W	• — —
K	— • —	X	— • • —
L	• — • •	Y	— • — —
M	— —	Z	— — • •

The full Morse code is based on combining dots and dashes to represent the letters of the alphabet.

• See page 48 SAMUEL MORSE

THE INVENTION OF THE POSTAGE STAMP

• In the early 1800s, postage in Britain was charged by distance and the number of sheets in a letter. The recipient paid for the postage not the sender.

• In 1837, retired English schoolteacher Rowland Hill wrote a pamphlet calling for cheap, standard postage rates, regardless of distance.

• The British Post Office took up Hill's ideas, and, in May 1840, issued the first adhesive postage stamps.

• The stamps were printed with black ink and become known as *Penny Blacks*.

POSTAGE ONE PENNY

PICTURE CAPTIONS
Captions explain the pictures.

JUST THE FACTS
Each topic box presents the facts you need in quick-to-read bullet points.

6–11 Inventions Timeline

46–51 Inventor Biographies

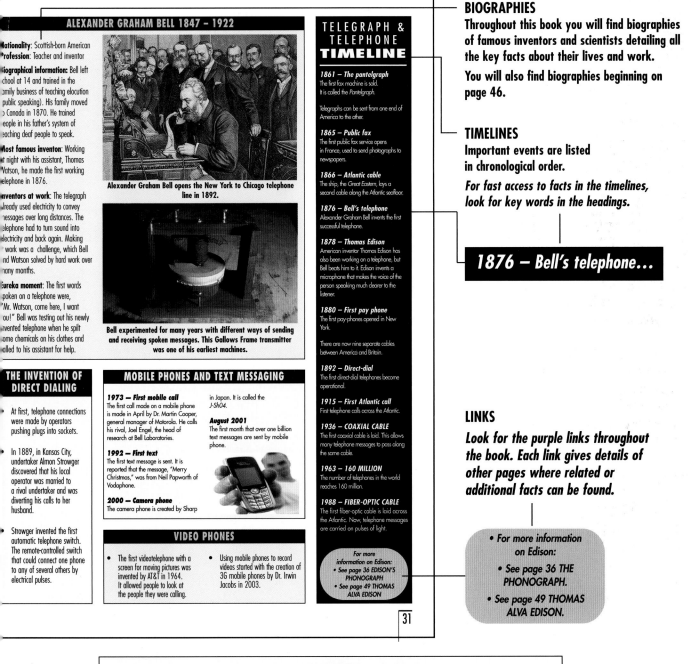

ALEXANDER GRAHAM BELL 1847 – 1922

Nationality: Scottish-born American

Profession: Teacher and inventor

Biographical information: Bell left school at 14 and trained in the family business of teaching elocution (public speaking). His family moved to Canada in 1870. He trained people in his father's system of teaching deaf people to speak.

Most famous invention: Working at night with his assistant, Thomas Watson, he made the first working telephone in 1876.

Inventors at work: The telegraph already used electricity to convey messages over long distances. The telephone had to turn sound into electricity and back again. Making it work was a challenge, which Bell and Watson solved by hard work over many months.

Eureka moment: The first words spoken on a telephone were, "Mr. Watson, come here, I want you!" Bell was testing out his newly invented telephone when he spilt some chemicals on his clothes and called to his assistant for help.

Alexander Graham Bell opens the New York to Chicago telephone line in 1892.

Bell experimented for many years with different ways of sending and receiving spoken messages. This Gallows Frame transmitter was one of his earliest machines.

THE INVENTION OF DIRECT DIALING

- At first, telephone connections were made by operators pushing plugs into sockets.

- In 1889, in Kansas City, undertaker Almon Strowger discovered that his local operator was married to a rival undertaker and was diverting his calls to her husband.

- Strowger invented the first automatic telephone switch. The remote-controlled switch that could connect one phone to any of several others by electrical pulses.

MOBILE PHONES AND TEXT MESSAGING

1973 – First mobile call
The first call made on a mobile phone is made in April by Dr. Martin Cooper, general manager of Motorola. He calls his rival, Joel Engel, the head of research at Bell Laboratories.

1992 – First text
The first text message is sent. It is reported that the message, "Merry Christmas," was from Neil Papworth of Vodaphone.

2000 – Camera phone
The camera phone is created by Sharp in Japan. It is called the J-Sh04.

August 2001
The first month that over one billion text messages are sent by mobile phone.

VIDEO PHONES

- The first videotelephone with a screen for moving pictures was invented by AT&T in 1964. It allowed people to look at the people they were calling.

- Using mobile phones to record videos started with the creation of 36 mobile phones by Dr. Irwin Jacobs in 2003.

TELEGRAPH & TELEPHONE TIMELINE

1861 – The pantelegraph
The first fax machine is sold. It is called the *Pantelegraph*.

Telegraphs can be sent from one end of America to the other.

1865 – Public fax
The first public fax service opens in France, used to send photographs to newspapers.

1866 – Atlantic cable
The ship, the *Great Eastern*, lays a second cable along the Atlantic seafloor.

1876 – Bell's telephone
Alexander Graham Bell invents the first successful telephone.

1878 – Thomas Edison
American inventor Thomas Edison has also been working on a telephone, but Bell beats him to it. Edison invents a microphone that makes the voice of the person speaking much clearer to the listener.

1880 – First pay phone
The first pay-phones opened in New York.

There are now nine separate cables between America and Britain.

1892 – Direct-dial
The first direct-dial telephones become operational.

1915 – First Atlantic call
First telephone calls across the Atlantic.

1936 – COAXIAL CABLE
The first coaxial cable is laid. This allows many telephone messages to pass along the same cable.

1963 – 160 MILLION
The number of telephones in the world reaches 160 million.

1988 – FIBER-OPTIC CABLE
The first fiber-optic cable is laid across the Atlantic. Now, telephone messages are carried on pulses of light.

For more information on Edison:
- See page 36 EDISON'S PHONOGRAPH
- See page 49 THOMAS ALVA EDISON

BIOGRAPHIES
Throughout this book you will find biographies of famous inventors and scientists detailing all the key facts about their lives and work.

You will also find biographies beginning on page 46.

TIMELINES
Important events are listed in chronological order.

For fast access to facts in the timelines, look for key words in the headings.

1876 – Bell's telephone...

LINKS
Look for the purple links throughout the book. Each link gives details of other pages where related or additional facts can be found.

- For more information on Edison:
- See page 36 THE PHONOGRAPH.
- See page 49 THOMAS ALVA EDISON.

GLOSSARY
- A **GLOSSARY** of words and terms used in this book begins on page 58.
The glossary words provide additional information to supplement the facts on the main pages.

AN AMAZING STORY

Ever since the Paleolithic people of the Stone Age invented simple tools for digging and cutting, inventions have changed the way human beings live. Our natural curiosity about the world around us has led us to search for more information about our planet and our ancestors. This timeline tracks the last 250,000 years and looks at some of the groundbreaking moments in human history.

c 250,000

STONE TOOLS
Paleolithic (Early Stone Age) human beings make simple stone tools, like hand axes, by flaking a piece of flint from a large stone then chipping away smaller flakes to create sharp edges for cutting.

What secrets are still to be discovered about our planet and our ancestors?

A flint hand axe, c 250,000

c 30,000 BC

BOWS AND ARROWS
Cave paintings from 30,000 BC onwards show Late Stone Age humans using bows and arrows to hunt animals. Hunters also use a variety of snares and traps.

THE FIRST CLOCKS

Long before there were clocks, people relied on regular, natural events to keep track of time. They worked, ate, and slept according to the rising of the sun. Over time, people invented many ways to track the passing of time.

WATER CLOCKS c AD 100
Water ran through this ancient Chinese *clepsydra*, or water clock, over a set period of time. As each section of the staircase-like timepiece emptied, people knew an exact amount of time had passed.

Water clock

CANDLE CLOCKS c AD 800
When candles were used for telling the time, they were often divided up into sections that each took an hour to burn.

SUNDIALS
For hundreds of years, people have used sundials to tell the time. The sundial's pointer casts a shadow onto a scale marked on the flat base. The scale shows the hours of the day.

PENDULUM CLOCKS
In the 1650s, there was a great breakthrough in timekeeping when a Dutch scientist, Christiaan Huygens built the first pendulum clock.

Huygens designed a mechanism that used the swing of a pendulum to control the rotation of weight-driven gearwheels inside the clock. This use of the pendulum had originally been thought of by mathematician Galileo Galilei.

• *See page 47 GALILEO GALILEI for information on Galileo and pendulums.*

Model of a Mesopotamian wheeled-vehicle, c 2000 BC.

c 3000 BC

WRITING
The Sumerians of southern Mesopotamia invent writing. Mesopotamian texts, still in existence today, range from simple lists to complex stories.

AD 200

ROMAN CENTRAL HEATING
The Romans heat using central heating systems called hypocausts. Heat from fires is drawn into an open space under the floor and then rises upward.

1400

CANNON
In Asia, bamboo-tube guns use gunpowder to shoot arrows. By AD 1400, metal cannons that fire stone cannonballs are in use across Europe.

1608

TELESCOPE
Hans Lippershey invents the telescope. Italian scientist, Galileo, builds his own telescope in 1609 and makes many new astronomical discoveries.

Galileo's telescope

Tool making dates back even further than this timeline, to *Homo habilis*, which means *handy man*, who lived 2 million years ago.

9000-7000 BC

FIRST FARMERS
People discover that domesticating animals, such as sheep and goats, gives a more regular meat supply than hunting. Cultivation of crops, such as wheat and barley, begins.

c 7000 BC

MAKING FIRE
Neolithic (Late Stone Age) people discover how to make fire by using simple tools fto produce friction and flints to cause sparks.

c 3500 BC

THE WHEEL
Wheels are first used in Mesopotamia (modern-day Iraq) as a turntable for making pottery. By 3500 BC, wheels are used on primative vehicles.

c 2500 BC

GLASS
Glass is made by heating sand with limestone and wood ash. The method for making glass is probably discovered by accident.

c 2000 BC

CHARIOTS
On the southwestern fringes of the Asia,the lightweight, two-wheeled, two-horse chariot develops. Chariots quickly become war vehicles in civilizations such as Egypt.

An ancient Egyptian wall carving showing a chariot.

c 1000 BC

GREEK ALPHABET
The ancient Greeks use a 24-letter alphabet adapted from the Phoenician alphabet. Each symbol in an alphabet represents a sound rather than a word.

1455

PRINTING PRESS
German Johannes Gutenberg develops movable type and designs and builds the first printing press. In 1455, Gutenberg prints his first book, a Latin bible.

A page from the Gutenberg Bible

THE ATOMIC CLOCK

The atomic clock was invented by English physicist Louis Essen in the 1950s.

- Atomic clocks use the energy changes that take place in atoms to keep track of time.

- Atomic clocks are so accurate they lose or gain no more than a second once every two or three millions years!

The US NBS–4 atomic clock.

1756

CHEMISTRY
The English scientist Joseph Black discovers the gas carbon dioxide when he notes that a substance in exhaled air combines with quicklime in a chemical reaction.

1772-1774

OXYGEN
Two scientists working independently discover oxygen—Swedish chemist Carl Wilhelm Scheele, around 1772, and English chemist Joseph Priestly in 1774.

1770s-1780s

STRUCTURE OF WATER
French chemist Antoine-Laurent Lavoisier discovers that water is a chemical combination of two gases (hydrogen and oxygen) that are found in air.

THE INVENTION OF PRINTING

Cai Lun (Ts'ai Lun) conceived the idea of forming sheets of paper from macerated tree bark, hemp waste, rags, and fishnets (c 100 BC) .

Without the invention of paper and printing, it would not have been possible to create this book!

c 1770 BC — Minoan printing
The Minoans invent the first known printing method. They use a writing system of 45 symbols, which are punched into a disk of clay before baking it.

c 200 BC — Punctuation
Punctuation came from Greek and Latin. Aristophanes of Byzantium, a librarian at the Library of Alexandria, is the first person to use punctuation. Early Greek writers did not even use spaces between words!

c 100 BC — Invention of paper
Cai Lun (Ts'ai Lun), a Chinese court official, is credited with the invention of paper.

c AD 350 — First book
Books with pages become the standard way of storing words.

c AD 600 — Block printing
Paper is pressed onto blocks on that text has either been carved or handwritten.

1455 — First movable type
German Johann Gutenberg invents a technique for mass-producing individual metal letters. The text is assembled letter by letter to make up a page. Then, oil-based ink is applied to the paper. The type is then reassembled for the next page.

1464 — Roman type
German printers Adolf Rusch, in 1464, and Sweynheim and Pannartz in 1465, seeking to avoid the heavy, spiky letters of early type, use a "roman" type, the forerunner of the type this book is printed in.

• See page 48
JOHANNES GUTENBERG

1794

COTTON
In the USA, Eli Whitney patents the cotton gin, a machine that combs the seeds out of cotton after it has been harvested.

Slaves work at a Whitney cotton gin.

The Locomotion pulled 28 coal-filled wagons on the new railway line.

1838-1839

CELLS
In 1838, German botanist Matthias Schleiden discovered that of cells. In 1839, Schleiden's friend, physiologist Theodor Schwann, proves that animals are also made up of cells.

1900

FINGERPRINTING
British scientist Francis Galton and police officer Sir Edward R. Henry devise a system of fingerprint classification that they publish in June. The Galton-Henry system is used in the UK for criminal identification starting in 1901.

A fingerprint

Wilbur and Orville Wright

1908

THE MODEL T
The first Model T car is produced by the Ford Motor Company. Revolutionary production methods will see 15 million Model T cars roll off the Ford assembly line over the next 19 years.

1927

EXPANDING UNIVERSE
Studying galaxies outside of the Milky Way, Edwin Hubble discovers that the galaxies seem to be moving away from the Milky Way. This leads to the theory that the universe is expanding.

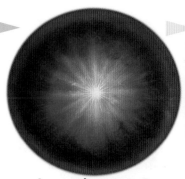

An expanding universe?

1796 ▶

VACCINATION
British doctor Edward Jenner develops the process of vaccination and successfully vaccinates a small boy against smallpox, a devastating disease in this period.

1822 ▶

MECHANICAL COMPUTER
Charles Babbage, an inventor and professor of mathematics, conceives the first mechanical computer.

1824 ▶

BRAILLE
Frenchman Louis Braille invents an alphabet tthat made use of rasied symbols that can be written and read by the blind. The alphabet has 63 characters.

1825

FIRST RAILWAY
The first railway in the world to carry freight and passengers using steam traction, the Stockton and Darlington Railway,, begins operation on September 27, in England.

An animal cell

1876 ▶

THE TELEPHONE
In March, Scottish-born American inventor Alexander Graham Bell is granted the patent for the telephone, a device that transmits speech sounds over electric wires.

1877 ▶

THE PHONOGRAPH
American inventor Thomas Edison invents the phonograph and records himself reciting the nursery rhyme, "Mary had a little lamb."

1882

FIRST POWER STATION
Thomas Edison supervises the laying of mains and installation of the world's first power station in New York City. It becomes operational in September.

1901 ▶

MARCONI'S MESSAGE
Italian physicist, Guglielmo Marconi creates a worldwide sensation when he successfully sends a radio message across the Atlantic Ocean on December 12. The message is dot dot dot, Morse code for the letter S.

1903

FIRST FLIGHT
The Wright brothers achieve the world's first powered flight with their "Flyer" biplane on December 17. The flight covers 120 feet and lasts just 12 seconds.

1913 ▶

ATOMIC STRUCTURE
Danish physicist Niels Bohr proposes his theory of atomic structure—that an atom consists of a nucleus surrounded by a cloud of orbiting electrons arranged in a series of concentric shells.

1926

TELEVISION
British television pioneer, John Logie Baird, demonstrates a television system. He presents fuzzy moving pictures of a face.

1941 ▶

PLUTONIUM (Pu)
The synthetic, radioactive element plutonium is made at Berkeley, California, by a team of scientists. Plutonium is used as an ingredient in nuclear weapons and as a fuel in some types of nuclear reactors.

1943

COLOSSUS
During World War II, Alan Turing and a team of British scientists secretly build Colossus, one of the first electronic computers, to decipher top secret messages created by the German Enigma coding machine.

THE INVENTION OF PHOTOGRAPHY

Thanks to the invention of photography, this book is filled with photographs of inventors and their inventions.

1826 - First photograph
In France, Joseph Niepce produces the world's first true photograph (as opposed to shadowgraph). The exposure time is about 8 hours.

1839 - Daguerreotype system
In France, Louis Daguerre demonstrates his daguerreotype system that produces a single positive image on a sheet of copper. Exposure time is 30 minutes.

1841 - Negatives
In England, William Talbot patents his calotype process that produces a negative image from which numerous positive copies can be made. Exposure time is 2–3 minutes.

1851 - Glass plates
In England, Frederick Archer introduces glass plates for photography. Exposure time is a few seconds.

1874 - Film roll
In the USA, George Eastman develops roll film, first using paper, later transparent celluloid. Exposure time is less than one second.

1888 - Kodak camera
Eastman launches the Kodak camera, which produces circular images.

1841 - First color film
In France, Auguste and Louis Lumière produce the first film for color transparencies.

1942 - First color prints
In Germany, the Agfa Company produces the first film for color prints.

1946 - Instant prints
In the USA, Edwin Land introduces a camera that makes instant prints.

A Daguerreotype camera.

• See page 49 GEORGE EASTMAN

Archaeologists can determine the age of this Egyptian mummy by using Willard F. Libby's discovery of the carbon dating process.

1946-1947 ▶

CARBON DATING

Willard F. Libby discovers that the unstable carbon isotope C14 decays over time to the more stable C12. This means that once-living things can be dated by the amount of C14 compared to C12 left in it.

1947

THE TRANSISTOR

William B. Shockley, John Bardeen, and Walter H. Brattain, invent the transistor— the device that will advance electronics and allow for the miniaturization of computer circuitry.

NUCLEAR POWER

FISSION

Fission is the process by which the nucleus of an atom is split in two releasing a large amount of energy. The fission of uranium atoms was first observed in the late 1930s.

CHAIN REACTION

On December 2, 1942, a team of scientists led by Enrico Fermi achieved the first controlled nuclear fission chain reaction.

MANHATTAN PROJECT

During World War II, a team of scientists in the USA worked on the top-secret Manhattan Project to design and build atom bombs. The first bomb was tested at Alamogordo Air Base, New Mexico on July 16,1945. In the following month, two atom bombs were dropped on the Japanese cities of Hiroshima and Nagasaki.

NUCLEAR ELECTRICITY

Uranium fission can be contained and controlled inside a reactor to produce heat for generating electricity. The first atomic power station making electricity for homes and businesses began operation in 1956 in England.

• See page 51 ENRICO FERMI.

1969 ▶

SUPERSONIC AIRLINER

On March 2, the Concorde, a passenger aircraft capable of flying at twice the speed of sound, makes its first test flight piloted by chief test pilot Andre Turcat.

Concorde

1983 ▶

HIV VIRUS

The HIV virus that causes AIDS is identified by French scientist Luc Montagnier and a team working at the Pasteur Institute in Paris.

1984

DNA PROFILING

Alec Jeffreys invents DNA profiling, a method of analyzing DNA to produce a set of characteristic features that are unique to each individual. The process can be used to identify criminals.

Alec Jeffreys

Dolly the sheep

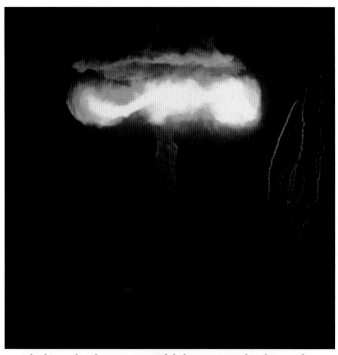

A hydrogen bomb (more powerful than an atom bomb) was first tested by the US in 1951.

2003 ▶

THE HUMAN GENOME

Human Genome Project completes the task of reading the human genome. The human genome is the set of instructions to build the body contained inside every cell.

1952

DNA DISCOVERIES

American biochemists Alfred Hershey and Martha Chase demonstrate that DNA transmits genetic information. In 1953, Crick and Watson unlock the structure of DNA.

DNA

1967

FIRST HEART TRANSPLANT

On December 3, a team, led by South African heart surgeon Christiaan Barnard, performs the world's first heart transplant in Cape Town, South Africa. The patient lives for 18 days.

1974

LUCY

Donald Johanson and Tom Gray discover the most complete Australopithecus skeleton ever found during excavations in northern Ethiopia. Nicknamed Lucy, this early hominid lived 3.2 million years ago.

1975

MICROSOFT

Bill Gates and Paul Allen start Microsoft. The company creates the operating system MS-DOS and Windows. These programs will eventually be used on almost every PC in the world.

Bill Gates

1991

WORLD WIDE WEB

Invented by British computer scientist Tim Berners-Lee in 1989, the World Wide Web is launched to the world via the Internet.

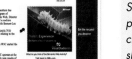

World Wide Web

1996

DOLLY THE SHEEP

A team of scientists working at the Roslin Institute in Scotland succeed in producing the first ever cloned mammal, Dolly, a sheep, on July 5.

2000

HUMAN GENOME DRAFT

A first draft of the human genome is published after more than 10 years of intensive effort. It consists of some three billion pairs of nucleotide bases divided into thousands of separate genes.

2004

A NEW PLANET

On March 15, NASA announces the discovery of Sedna, possibly a new planet. Its diameter is 110 miles.

Sedna takes over 10,000 years to orbit the sun. Many scientists do not yet agree that Sedna is a planet.

DEVELOPMENTS IN MATHEMATICS

Place Value

The use of "0" for zero dates from c AD 500. This marks the emergence of the decimal system we use.

Decimal fraction

Though used in China in c AD 200 these were not developed in other parts of the world until c 1300–1400.

Algebra

The word *algebra* comes from a book by Al-Khwarizmi, an Arab mathematician who lived c AD 780–850. The most famous algebraic equation is Einstein's:

$$E=mc^2$$

Imperial measures

Standard Imperial Units of distance (for example, the mile) were set by Queen Elizabeth I in 1592.

Statistics

Beginning around 1654, Blaise Pascal, a French mathematician, began to work on a theory of probability (the chance of something happening).

Metric measures

The meter, liter, and gram were adopted by the French in 1795.

Pythagoras' theorem

Pythagoras lived c 580–500 BC. His theorem says that the square drawn using the longest side of a right angle triangle is equal in area to the sum of the areas of the triangles on the other two sides. This theorem is used in navigation, maps, building, and land measurement.

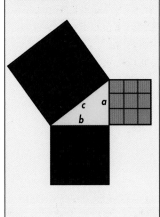

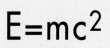

INVENTION TIMELINE

c 35,000 BC – Advanced stone tools

Burins, engraving tools made from a flint with a sharp edge, are used to decorate bone and wooden items.

Wooden handles are attached to stone tools for the first time making it possible to hit things harder and to increase the amount of swing achieved with a tool, such as an axe.

c 30,000 BC – Rope

Rope made from plant fibers is used for making nets and snares for catching animals.

c 9000 BC – First ovens

The first known ovens, stone or clay chambers heated by a fire, are in use in Jericho in ancient Palestine.

c 8000 BC – Flint mining

When people can no longer find enough flints on the ground around them for tool-making, they begin to mine or dig for stones under the surface.

c 7000 BC – Flax and linen

The flax plant is cultivated for its fibers that can be used to make ropes and linen.

c 6000 BC – Axe heads

Stones are shaped to create axe heads with straight, sharp edges and heavy bases.

c 5500 BC – Weaving

The weaving of baskets develops: split bamboo is used in China, straw and flax in the Middle East, and willow in Europe.

c 5000 BC – Leather

Animal are dried and preserved using substances, such as urine.

c 5000 BC – Grindstones

Grindstones, two stones that fit together, are used to crush cereal grains. This produces flour that is easier to digest than whole grains.

• See page 6 STONE TOOLS
• The TIMELINE continues on page 13.

EARLY INVENTORS

Over thousands of years, early human beings invented and discovered ways to make their lives more efficient. They developed farming to ensure a regular supply of food, and they devised tools and simple machines to make work easier. They also conceived ways of recording their lives, such as painting and writing, without which it would be impossible to chart the history of human invention and discovery.

EARLY FARMING INVENTIONS AND DISCOVERIES

5000 BC – Scratch plow
The wooden scratch plough is used for breaking up the soil. The scratch plows are probably pulled by donkeys.

4000 BC – Sickle
Bone-handled sickles with a flint blade are used to reap wheat and barley.

3000 BC – Shaduf
Egyptians use a shaduf (a bucket on a weighted pole) to lift water from irrigation canals to water their crops.

2000 BC – Pollination
The discovery that there are male and female plants makes it easier to select crops for size, taste, and disease-resistance by artificial pollination.

AD 500 – Three-piece plows
Heavy, iron, three-piece plows come into use. They usually have wheels and are pulled by large farm horses. The plow helps farmers to work heavier soils and plow faster.

AD 500 – Horse collar
The creation of the horse collar enables a horse to pull a heavy plough without choking.

AD 800 – Crop rotation
In northeastern France, the crop rotation system is developed. One field is planted in autumn with winter wheat or rye; the second field is planted the following spring with barley, peas, or oats (to feed horses); the third field is left fallow. This allows more of the field to be cultivated and improves the soil.

AD 900 – Horseshoe
The horseshoe enables horses to pull ploughs for longer periods.

• See page 7 FIRST FARMERS

This ancient Egyptian wooden model dates to around 2000 BC. It shows a farmer using a simple scratch plough pulled by oxen.

DISCOVERING AND INVENTING METAL

Archaeologists study metal artifacts to determine when ancient civilizations first discovered metals such as bronze and iron.

COPPER 8000–6500 BC
The discovery of copper gives early human beings a practical substitute for stone. Copper is easy to shape.

LEAD 6500 BC
Early metalworkers extract lead by heating lead ore in a hot fire. Decorative lead beads found in Turkey suggest that lead was considered a precious material.

BRONZE 3500 BC
Ancient metalworkers melt copper and tin together and create a new metal, called *bronze*. This new material is used to make weapons and decorative items.

IRON 2000 BC
Iron is extracted from iron ore (stone containing iron) by heating the ore in red-hot charcoal. Iron is hard to melt, so early metalworkers develop new techniques such as hammering hot iron into the required shape.

THE INVENTION OF WRITING

THE FIRST WRITING

The Sumerians (who lived in what is now southern Iraq) had invented writing by around 3000 BC. They used a piece of reed to make cuneiform symbols (wedge-shaped marks) in clay tablets. Then, they baked the tablets to harden them.

HIEROGLYPHS

The ancient Egyptians also developed writing soon after 3000 BC. They used hundreds of pictures, called *hieroglyphs,* to represent words and sounds. They carved inscriptions on temple walls, painted on the walls of tombs, and wrote on papyrus paper.

CHINESE PICTOGRAMS

The ancient Chinese began writing around 1700 BC. They used a different pictogram (symbol) to represent each word. There were thousands of pictograms.

• See page 6
THE GREEK ALPHABET

THE INVENTION OF PAINTING

Ancient paintings dating to around 30,000 BC have been found in caves in western Europe.

Prehistoric artists invented painting using paint made from minerals, such as chalk and red iron oxide. They made simple brushes made from chewed twigs or animal hair and lamps that burned animal fat to light the dark interiors of the caves where they worked.

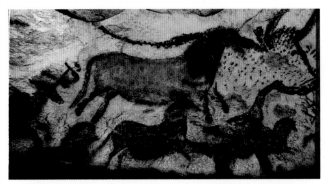

The artworks in the Lascaux caves in France (above) have been dated to around 15,000 BC.

LASCAUX CAVE PAINTINGS

The discovery: Caves containing over 2000 prehistoric paintings and engravings.
Discovered: September 12, 1940
Discovered by: Marcel Ravidat, Jacques Marsal, Georges Agnel and Simon Coencas, four teenage boys exploring in woods near Montignac in France.

INVENTION OF POTTERY

c 13,000 BC
The first potters discover they can make useful containers by shaping soft clay by hand, then heating it in a fire to bake it hard.

c 6500 BC
Thin layers of colored clay, called *slip,* and natural pigments, such as red ochre, are used to decorate pottery. Examples of this innovation have been found in the ancient city of Catal Huyuk (now Cumra in Turkey).

4000–3000 BC
The Mesopotamian potters invent the potter's wheel. This wheel uses a slowly spinning stone wheel to produce pots with a uniform shape.

A Mesopotamian vase from 3400–3200 BC.

PAPYRUS PAPER

The ancient Egyptians invented papyrus, a type of paper made from papyrus reeds that grew by the River Nile.

Fibers from the reeds were squashed together into flat sheets and dried in the sun.

A papyrus reed

INVENTION TIMELINE

c 4000 BC – Scales
Simple scales (a length of wood or metal balanced with pans hung from each end) are developed in Mesopotamia.

C 4000 BC – Gold/silver
Gold and silver are discovered. They are used for making ornaments and as a means of exchange for goods or service.

c 3500 BC – Bricks
In the Middle East, bricks are made from clay, then fired in a kiln to make them hard and waterproof. Prior to this, bricks were made from mud and straw, but they sometimes melted in heavy rain.

c 3000 BC – Cotton
Cotton fabric is invented. People of the Indus Valley (modern-day Pakistan) discover that the silky fibers attached to the seeds of the cotton plant can be woven into a fine fabric.

c 2600 BC – Chairs
The ancient Egyptians use chairs with padded seats and four legs. (Ancient people had probably used many objects to sit on before this time, but chairs as we recognize them today have been found in ancient Egyptian tombs from this period.)

c 2500 BC – Ink/mirrors
Ink for writing is made from soot mixed with glue. Mirrors made from discs of polished bronze or copper are used in ancient Egypt.

c 2000 BC – Wheel spokes
Mesopotamian craftsmen begin to produce wheels with a rim, hub, and spokes instead of the heavy, solid plank-wheels previously used.

c 1500 BC – Flags
Flags are invented in China and used in battles. If a leader's flag is captured by the enemy, it means the enemy has won the battle.

c 600 BC – Rotary querns
The rotary quern is invented. For over 4000 years, corn has been ground by hand using two stones. The rotary quern is a circular stone that fits into a stone base. The top stone is turned by a wooden handle crushing the grain between the two stones. It is also known as a *hand mill.*

NATURAL WORLD

Human beings have searched to know more about their origins and Earth. Today, we know our planet is 4.5 billion years old, not the 74,832 years proposed by the French scientist Buffon in 1778. Paleontologists have discovered and identified the first animals that lived on Earth. Anthropologists have studied the fossils of our earliest ancestors. Scientists have discovered that all plants and animals are made from cells; we now know that DNA within those cells is the blueprint for all living things.

Fossil hunter William Buckland (1784–1856)

DISCOVERING THE DINOSAURS

DINOSAUR FOSSILS
- In the 1820s, Mary Anning began a career as a professional fossil collector on the shores of Lyme Regis in England. Anning supplied scientists of the period with their fossils. During her career, she discovered the fossils of *plesiosaurs*, *ichthyosaurs*, and the first *pterosaur*.

This illustration of an *ichthyosaur* is based on fossil finds.

A *Megalosaurus* jawbone

THE FIRST DINOSAUR
- Fossils of a jawbone and teeth were found in Oxfordshire, England, around 1815.

- William Buckland studied the fossils that he believed were from a large, meat-eating reptile.

- In 1822, Buckland's colleague James Parkinson named the creature *Megalosaurus*, meaing *big lizard*.

INVENTING DINOSAURS
- In 1842, English scientist Sir Richard Owen invented the term *dinosauria* to describe the *Megalosaurus* and two other fossil animals, *Iguanodon* and *Hylaeosaurus*, found at the time.

THE FIRST BIRD
- In 1860, 1861, and 1877, the fossils of a single feather and of two birds were discovered in the same Jurassic limestone quarry in Solnhofen, Germany. The bird was named *Archaeopteryx*. It seemed to be a transition form between dinosaurs and birds.

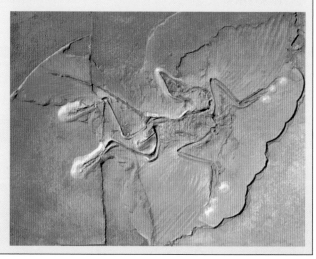

An *Archaeopteryx* fossil

CHARLES DARWIN

- Scientist Charles Darwin was intrigued by the variety of bird species he observed in the Galapagos Islands.

- In 1837, when ornithologist John Gould showed that the islands' birds were all closely related finches, despite their differences, it led Darwin to suggest that the various forms had evolved from a single species.

- In 1859, Darwin published *On the Origin of Species,* a book presenting the theory that animals and plants have not always looked the way they do today, but have evolved from earlier forms, and are still evolving.

HOMO ERECTUS

The discovery:
The remains of a skull cap and some teeth with features similar to those of both apes and humans. Found in caves in Java, Indonesia. Nicknamed "Java man."

Discovered by:
Dutch paleontologist, Eugene Dubois in 1891.

Homo erectus skull

Discovery fact:
The first known fossils to be discovered of *homo erectus.*

- See page 11
LUCY (1974)

CONTINENTAL DRIFT

- In 1912, German meteorologist Alfred Wegener proposed that the world's continents were once joined together in a single, large landmass he called *Pangaea.*

- Over millions of years, the individual continents had drifted apart, but it is still possible to see how they may have fitted together.

- Wegener's discovery of continental drift was finally accepted by scientists in the 1960s.

TIMELINE

1902 – Chromosomes
American surgeon Walter Sutton discovers the *chromosome theory of inheritance.* He believes that Mendel's features were controlled in living cells by structures called *chromosomes.* The chemical messages encoded in the chromosomes are the genes.

1909 – Burgess Shale
American paleontologist Charles Walcott discovers the Burgess Shale fossil site in Canada's Rocky Mountains. Dating from the Cambrian period, it contains thousands of fossils of marine animals.

1927 – Big Bang
Belgian priest Georges Lemaitre proposes a forerunner of the Big Bang theory: that the universe began with the explosion of a primeval atom.

1953 – Age of the Earth
Fiesel Houtermans and Claire Patterson use radiometric dating to date the Earth at 4.5 billion years old.

1963 – Plate tectonics
Fred Vine and Drummond Matthews discover seafloor spreading. This leads to the establishment of plate tectonics.

1964 – Big Bang
Arno Penzias and Robert Wilson detect cosmic radiation (radiation coming from space) and use it to confirm the Big Bang Theory.

1980 – Dinosaur extinction
Luis and Walter Alvarez put forward the *asteroid impact theory* of dinosaur extinction.

1985 – Ozone depletion
Scientists of the British Antarctic Survey discover the depletion of ozone in the upper atmosphere.

1991 – Asteroid impact
Chicxulub crater in Yucatán is pinpointed as the site of the asteroid impact that caused dinosaur extinction.

- See the GLOSSARY for explanations of many of the scientific terms used in this timeline.

THE STORY OF DNA

1869 - DNA discovered
Swiss graduate chemist Johann Miescher identifies a particular substance, deoxyribonucleic acid (DNA), in the nuclei of white blood cells. The importance of this discovery goes unnoticed for more than 50 years.

1929 - DNA molecule
In the USA, Russian-born chemist Phoebus Levene establishes that the DNA molecule is composed of a series of nucleotides. Each one is composed of a sugar, a phosphate group, and one of four bases: thymine (T), guanine (G), cytosine (C), and adenine (A).

1950 - Base pairs
In the USA, biochemist Erwin Chargaff discovers that the bases are arranged in pairs, and that the composition of DNA is identical within species, but differs between species.

1952 - Genetic code
Two American scientists, Alfred Hershey and Martha Chase, conduct an experiment proving that the DNA molecule is how genetic information is transmitted.

1952 - DNA analysis
In England, scientists Maurice Wilkins and Rosalind Franklin analyze the DNA molecule using X-rays.

1953 - Shape of DNA
Wilkins' and Franklin's results enable the shape of the DNA molecule to be determined by Frances Crick and James Watson.

1965 - Cell proteins
American biochemist Marshall Nirenberg deciphers the genetic code through which DNA controls the production of proteins inside body cells.

1983 - Polymerase chain reaction
American researcher Kary Mullis invents the polymerase chain reaction (PCR), a laboratory process that enables scientists to duplicate small sections of the DNA molecule many millions of times in a short period of time.

- See page 51 FRANCIS CRICK AND JAMES WATSON
- See the GLOSSARY for scientific terms used in this timeline.

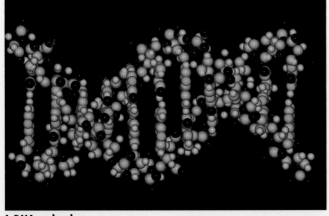

A DNA molecule

• *See page 12*
DISCOVERING AND INVENTING METAL

SCIENCE ALL AROUND

Science is the close observation of nature. Although many scientists now use sophisticated equipment such as lasers and hadron colliders, their basic technique is the same as taught in every school science class: observe, investigate, understand, and describe. Potential new discoveries are all around us. For example, an amazing new form of carbon that scientists had previously thought impossible was recently discovered in some dirty residue that had built up around an old electric lamp.

THE PERIODIC TABLE

In 1869, Russian chemist Dmitri Meldeleev discovered that the elements can be placed in ascending sequence of atomic size, arranged across a periodic table of rows and columns. Elements with similar physical or chemical properties are located near to each other.

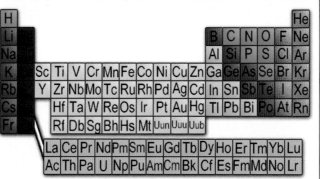

Meldeleev's original periodic table had gaps that predicted the existence of undiscovered elements. These gaps have since been filled.

THE INVENTION OF THE MICROSCOPE

THE FIRST MICROSCOPE
In the Netherlands, in 1668, Anton van Leeuwenhoek constructed the first working microscope.
It had a small, convex lens and could magnify around 200 times the original size. The entire instrument was only 4 inches long. The user held it up to the eye.

DISCOVERING BACTERIA
In 1674, Van Leeuwenhoek was the first person to observe protozoa from ponds. In 1676, he examined bacteria from his own mouth.

VAN LEEWENHOEK'S MICROSCOPE

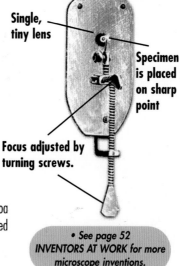

Single, tiny lens

Specimen is placed on sharp point

Focus adjusted by turning screws.

• *See page 52*
INVENTORS AT WORK for more microscope inventions.

A NEW CARBON

In 1985, three university professors jointly discovered new form of the carbon molecule.

Instead of just four atoms, like other forms of carbon, it has 60 atoms arranged in a hollow, multisided, geometric shape. The new substance, which is incredibly strong for its weight, has been named *buckminsterfullerene*, and the hollow shapes are known as *buckyballs*.

HIGH ENERGY COLLISIONS

To study the structure of atoms, scientists build massive devices that use magnetism to accelerate bits of atomic nuclei so that they crash into each other at very high speed and break apart.
The first such device, called a *cyclotron*, was built in the USA in 1933. The latest device, known as a *Large Hadron Collider*, is located on the border between France and Switzerland.

LASERS

WHAT IS A LASER?

In a laser, a crystal or gas is energized so that its atoms start to emit light. The light produced by a laser is of nearly uniform wavelength and the light rays are almost perfectly parallel so that there is very little spreading of the beam.

THE FIRST LASER

In 1960, scientist Theodore Maiman built the first laser (Light Amplification by Stimulated Emission of Radiation). It used a rod-shaped crystal of synthetic ruby to produce a very bright, very narrow beam of light. Gas lasers were invented a few months after the ruby laser.

An experiment showing an intense ruby laser beam penetrating two prisms.

LASER BEAMS ON THE MOON

In the 1970s, lasers were used to measure the exact distance between the Earth and the moon. The narrow beam of a laser was bounced off reflectors which had been put on the moon's surface by Apollo astronauts.

LASERS ALL AROUND

Today, tiny semiconductor devices smaller than a pinhead produce the laser light that reads the digital information encoded onto CDs and DVDs.

1800 – First battery
Italian physicist Alessandro Volta invents the first electric battery. It uses chemical reactions to produce an electric current.

1807 – Electrolysis
English scientist Humphry Davy invents the process of extracting metals from minerals by electrolysis. He heats the minerals to melting point and then applies an electric current to extract the metal.

1820 – Ampere's Law
French scientist Andre Ampere experiments with magnets and electricity and discovers the mathematical relationship between magnetism and the flow of electrical current.

1827 – Ohm's law
In Germany, the physicist Georg Ohm discovers the relationship between resistance and current in an electrical circuit.

1831 – Induction
English scientist Michael Faraday discovers the laws of induction that explain how a variable magnetic field causes electrical current to flow through copper wires—the principle behind both the electric generator and the electric motor.

1864 – Electricity and magnetism
Scottish mathematician James Maxwell discovers four basic equations that describe all the relationships between electricity and magnetism.

1888 – First generator
Croatian inventor Nikola Tesla designs the world's first successful alternating current (AC) generator. Alternating current is more powerful than the direct current (DC) produced by batteries.

1947 – The transistor
In America, electrical engineers invent the transistor, the world's first semiconductor device, beginning the Electronic Age.

> • See the GLOSSARY for a detailed definition of a SEMICONDUCTOR DEVICE.

THE STORY OF GENETIC ENGINEERING

> • See page 14 TIMELINE for Gregor Mendel's discovery of heredity.

1954 - GENETIC CODE
Russian physicist George Gamow is the first to suggest that the DNA bases T, G, C, and A form a genetic code that looks like CGCTGACATCGT, etc.

1966 - FROG CLONING
In England, biologist John Gurdon clones frogs from cells taken from the intestines of a tadpole.

1971 - RESTRICTION ENZYMES
In the USA, molecular biologists Daniel Nathans and Hamilton Smith discover restriction enzymes that can be used to cut the DNA molecule into short strands.

1972 - RECOMBINANT DNA
American scientist Patrick Berg succeeds in splicing together strands of DNA to produce recombinant DNA (DNA that has been recombined from a number of different strands). This marks the beginning of true genetic engineering.

1994 - GM CROPS
In the USA, a rot-resistant tomato becomes the first genetically modified (GM) crop to be approved for sale to the public.

1996 - CLONED MAMMAL
In Scotland, a team of scientists led by Ian Wilmut succeed in producing Dolly the sheep, the world's first cloned mammal.

Dolly the cloned sheep had no immediate practical value, but the cloning technique is vital. If, for example, scientists can genetically engineer a cow to produce milk that contains life-saving drugs, then they can use the cloning technique to make thousands of identical cows.

> • See page 15 THE STORY OF DNA
> • See the GLOSSARY for scientific terms used in this timeline.

MAKING DOLLY THE SHEEP
- The nucleus was removed from an unfertilized egg.
- Next, a cell from an adult sheep was fused with the egg by passing an electric current through the two.
- They became one cell which then behaved like a fertilized egg and began to divide.
- Finally, the cell was implanted into another female sheep where it developed normally into an embryo.

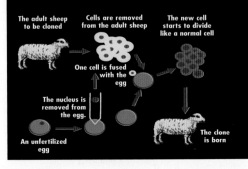

The adult sheep to be cloned

Cells are removed from the adult sheep

The new cell starts to divide like a normal cell

One cell is fused with the egg

The nucleus is removed from the egg.

An unfertilized egg

The clone is born

Dr. Ian Wilmut and Dolly the sheep.

EXPLORING SPACE

DISCOVERY TIMELINE

1543 – Sun-centered universe
Polish astronomer Copernicus publishes *Six Books Concerning the Revolutions of the Heavenly Orbs* that presents his discoveries and theory of the universe with the Sun at the center.

1609 – Galileo's telescope
Galileo hears of Lippershey's invention and builds his own telescope. He uses his new instrument to make many discoveries, including Jupiter's four largest moons and sunspots from which he deduces that the Sun rotates.

1610 – Orion Nebula
Frenchman Nicolas-Claude Fabri de Peiresc discovers the Orion Nebula. This star "nursery" is visible with the naked eye. Stars are being born there right now.

1705 – Halley's Comet
Edmond Halley discovers that comets observed in 1531, 1607, and 1682 are the same comet. He predicts the comet will return in 1758. The comet is sighted in that year (after Halley's death) and is named in his honor.

1922–1924 New galaxies
American astronomer Edwin Hubble discovers that there are other galaxies outside of our galaxy, the Milky Way.

1931 – Radio waves from space
American engineer Karl Jansky is assigned by Bell Telephone Laboratories, in New Jersey, to track down interference which is causing problems to telephone communications. Jansky finds all the sources except one. After months of study, he establishes that the radio interference is coming from the stars.

1995 – Hale-Bopp comet
US amateur astronomers Alan Hale in New Mexico and Thomas Bopp in Arizona independently discover a new comet on July 23. At its brightest in 1997, Hale-Bopp was a thousand times brighter than Halley's comet.

When the telescope was invented in the 17th century, astronomers were able to study the stars and the planets in more detail. In the early 20th century, pioneering rocket scientists, such as Konstantin Tsiolovsky, Robert Goddard, Herman Oberth, and Werner von Braun, expanded our horizons further when they developed the means to blast a satellite, or a human being, into space.

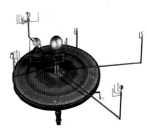

The orrery, a mechanical model of our solar system, invented in the mid 1700s.

ROCKET PIONEERS

1150 – Chinese rockets
Gunpowder propelled rockets are invented by the Chinese.

c 1900 – Tsiolkovsky
Russian scientist Konstantin Tsiolkovsky suggests using rockets with stages that can be jettisoned to get large objects into space.

1926 – Goddard's Rocket
American Robert Goddard experiments with different fuels. In 1926, the first rocket to use a liquid propellant was launched from Goddard's Aunt Effie's cabbage patch.

Goddard's work earns him the nickname, "Father of Modern Rocketry."

1920s–1930s
German Herman Oberth develops much of the modern theory for rocket and spaceflight. German scientist Werner von Braun produces the V2 rocket (a weapon) for Germany in WWII, then goes to America to work on the space program.

INVENTION OF THE TELESCOPE

HANS LIPPERSHEY
Dutch spectacle-maker Hans Lippershey is credited with inventing the refracting telescope in 1608. Lippershey discovered that if you look through two lenses of the right type, they will enlarge distant objects.

Lippershey offered his new "looker" to the government for use in warfare. He was paid 900 florins for the instrument, but there was a requirement that it be modified into a binocular device.

REFRACTING TELESCOPES
Refracting telescopes work by having a convex lens which bends light rays from an object to form an upside-down image of the object. A second lens, the eyepiece, bends the rays again and magnifies the image.

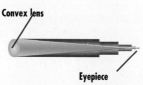

Convex lens

Eyepiece

Newton's telescope

NEWTON'S TELESCOPE
In 1668, English mathematician Isaac Newton developed the reflecting telescope. English astronomer John Gregory had thought up an alternative reflector design in 1663.

REFLECTING TELESCOPES
A reflecting telescope uses a shaped primary mirror to reflect light to a smaller secondary mirror. The light is then reflected to the focus and the image is viewed through an eyepiece.

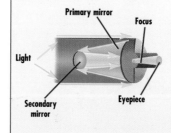

Primary mirror

Focus

Light

Secondary mirror

Eyepiece

RADIO TELESCOPES
Radio telescopes receive radio waves emitted by objects in space and, through a computer, convert those waves to images. Radio waves can penetrate through dust clouds that block visible light.

• See page 19 1931 – RADIO WAVES FROM SPACE

SOLAR SYSTEM DISCOVERIES

Some of the planets in our solar system have been known for many years, while others were discovered more recently. Both astronomers on Earth and space probes have added to the long list of solar system discoveries.

JUPITER – GREAT RED SPOT
Jupiter's Great Red Spot (GRS) was discovered by the French astronomer, Gian Domenico Cassini, in 1665 using an early telescope.

Thanks to space probes we now know the GRS is around 7,500 miles by 15,5000 miles and is a vast, violent storm.

VENUS – VOLCANOES
Following the mapping of Venus's surface by NASA's *Magellan* probe (1990–1994), scientists discovered that Venus is covered in volcanoes, including an active volcano Maat Mons. Venus and Earth are the only two planets known to have active volcanoes.

MERCURY – CRATERS
When Mercury was first photographed by the NASA probe *Mariner 10* in 1974, it was discovered that Mercury has many deep craters. The largest, the Caloris Basin, is around 800 miles across.

PLUTO
Pluto's existence had been predicted by astronomer Percival Lowell, but it was actually discovered by American Clyde Tombaugh at the Lowell Observatory in 1930.

In 1978, Pluto's close satellite, Charon, was discovered by James Walter Christy.

Pluto

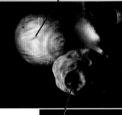

Charon

URANUS
Sir William Herschel discovered Uranus on March 13, 1781, using a home-made reflecting telescope that was about 6.5 feet long. Herschel originally thought Uranus was a comet.

NEPTUNE
Neptune was discovered in 1846 by astronomer J.G. Gale in Berlin. Neptune's position had been predicted by the mathematicians John Couch Adams in England and Urbain Le verrier in France.

MARS - CRATERS
In 1971, the space probe Mariner 9 discovered a system of canyons known as the Valles Marineris. The canyons stretch for around 2500 miles. Some individual canyons are 100 km wide and some are 5–6 miles deep.

MARS - VOLCANOES
The largest volcano in the solar system, Olympus Mons, was discovered on Mars. It is 16 miles high. The tallest volcano on Earth, Mauna Loa in Hawaii, rises 6 miles above the ocean floor.

SATURN – THE RINGS
Saturn's ring system was discovered by Galileo in 1610. Galileo's primitive telescope could not make out the structure of the rings. We now know that the rings are made of millions of small chunks of rock and ice.

MARS - MOONS
In 1877, the American astronomer Asaph Hall discovered Mars' two moons. He named them *Phobos* and *Deimos* after the sons of Ares, the Greek counterpart of the Roman god Mars.

Some scientists believed this rod-like structure to be a fossilized, microscopic Martian creature.

IT CAME FROM SPACE
We all benefit from inventions developed by NASA for space missions.

- Battery-powered tools were invented for use in space where there are no electrical sockets.

- The digital watch was invented to help astronauts keep accurate time.

- Plastic sandwich boxes were originally used to keep food for astronauts fresh.

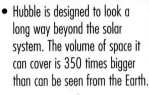

HUBBLE SPACE TELESCOPE

The Hubble Space Telescope is a satellite built by NASA and ESA. It was launched in 1990 and orbits about 350 miles above the Earth.

- The telescope is named after astronomer Edwin Hubble.

- Hubble is a reflecting telescope, and it also works in ultraviolet. It is powered by two solar panels.

- Hubble is designed to look a long way beyond the solar system. The volume of space it can cover is 350 times bigger than can be seen from the Earth.

LIFE ON MARS
In 1996, US geologist David S. Mckay and a team from NASA's Johnson Space Center in Houston reported that they had found evidence of microscopic life on Mars. The tiny microbes were found inside a meteorite which had travelled from Mars to Earth possibly taking millions of years. At present, many scientists do not agree with McKay's findings.

HUMAN BODY

DISCOVERY TIMELINE

AD 200 – Galen
Greek-born doctor Claudius Galen describes the workings of the body. Galen's work is often based on animal dissections. His findings, many incorrect, remain unchallenged until the 1500s.

1543 – Vesalius's anatomy
Flemish doctor Andreas Vesalius publishes the first accurate description of human anatomy, *De humani corporis fabrica libri septem* (*The Seven books of the Human Body*). It is based on his dissections of human cadavers.

1614 – Santorio
Italian physician Santorio Santorio completes 30 years of research experimenting on his own body to see how it works.

1800 – Cells
French doctor Marie-François Bichat shows that organs are made of different groups of cells, called *tissues*.

1889 – Neurons
Spanish physiologist Ramón Santiago y Cajal discovers that the nervous system is made up of neurons that do not touch.

1905 – Hormones
British physiologists William Bayliss and Ernest Starling invent the term *hormone* to describe the newly-discovered "chemical messengers" that control many body activities.

1912 – Vitamins
Polish-American biochemist Casimir Funk invents the term *vitamin* to describe nutrients required by the body in tiny amounts to make it work properly.

1970s – Natural painkillers
Discovery that natural painkillers, called *enkephalins* and *endorphins*, are produced by the body.

• See page 15 **THE STORY OF DNA**
• See page 17 **THE STORY OF GENETIC ENGINEERING**

Most body activities, including how we move and digest food, are now well understood thanks to discoveries made in the past 500 years. The earliest anatomists studied the structure of body organs, such as the heart and kidneys. Later, physiologists discovered how these organs worked. There are still discoveries being made today. The Human Genome Project, for example, having read the DNA in our cells, is now identifying the instructions in our DNA needed to build and run a human being.

Anatomist Andreas Vesalius (1514–1564)

DISCOVERY TIMELINE: BLOOD

1628 - Blood circulation
British doctor William Harvey's experiments prove that blood circulates through the body, pumped by the heart, in blood vessels.

1658 - Red blood cells
Red blood cells are first observed and identified by Dutch naturalist Jan Swammerdam using an early microscope.

1661 - Blood capillaries
The existence of blood capillaries—tiny blood vessels that link arteries to veins—is discovered by Italian microscopist Marcello Malpighi.

1884 - Action of white blood cells
Russian zoologist Elie Metchnikoff describes how white blood cells surround and devour bacteria and other germs.

1901 - Blood groups
The existence of blood groups is discovered by Austrian-American doctor Karl Landsteiner. The four blood groups are later named *A*, *B*, *AB*, and *O*. Blood transfusions will only work if the right type of blood is given. Landsteiner's discoveries allow for safe blood transfusions.

1959 - Hemoglobin structure
Scientist Max Perutz discovers the structure of hemoglobin, the substance inside red blood cells that carries oxygen and makes those cells red.

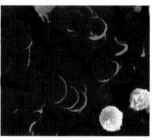

Blood cells

THE HUMAN GENOME PROJECT

• In the late 1980s, groups of scientists around the world set out on an unprecedented research project—to produce a map of the human genome, or human genetic code.

• Several anonymous donors provided DNA for the project. The resulting DNA map will be typical of all human DNA.

• In 2000, scientists released a rough draft of the human genome showing all of the estimated 3 billion base pairs in human DNA.

• In April 2003, the Human Genome Project completed the map, giving scientists the ability, for the first time, to read the complete genetic blueprint for building a human.

• It will take decades to understand what all of the 25,000 to 30,000 human genes do, but scientists hope that new treatments and earlier diagnosis of diseases will be among the many benefits of this vast and pioneering project.

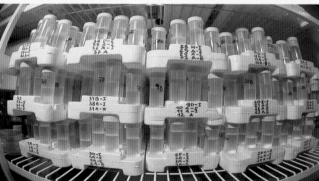

Phials containing every gene in the human body from the Human Genome Project.

• See the GLOSSARY for explanations of many of the scientific terms used in this timeline.

DISCOVERING THE HUMAN BODY

The human body is made up of 10 trillion cells of 200 different types. It has taken hundreds of years to understand how it works, and there are still more discoveries to be made.

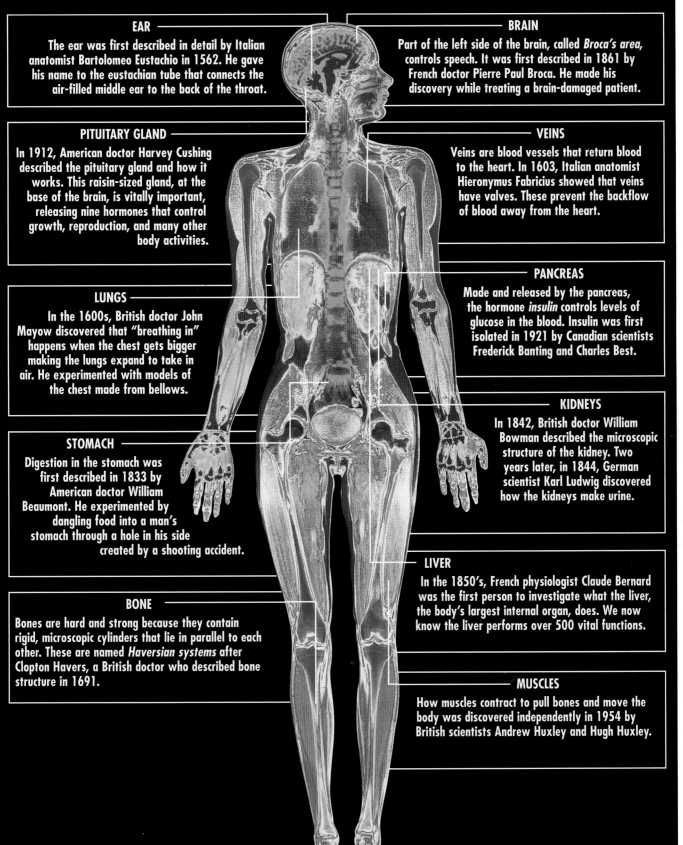

EAR
The ear was first described in detail by Italian anatomist Bartolomeo Eustachio in 1562. He gave his name to the eustachian tube that connects the air-filled middle ear to the back of the throat.

BRAIN
Part of the left side of the brain, called *Broca's area*, controls speech. It was first described in 1861 by French doctor Pierre Paul Broca. He made his discovery while treating a brain-damaged patient.

PITUITARY GLAND
In 1912, American doctor Harvey Cushing described the pituitary gland and how it works. This raisin-sized gland, at the base of the brain, is vitally important, releasing nine hormones that control growth, reproduction, and many other body activities.

VEINS
Veins are blood vessels that return blood to the heart. In 1603, Italian anatomist Hieronymus Fabricius showed that veins have valves. These prevent the backflow of blood away from the heart.

LUNGS
In the 1600s, British doctor John Mayow discovered that "breathing in" happens when the chest gets bigger making the lungs expand to take in air. He experimented with models of the chest made from bellows.

PANCREAS
Made and released by the pancreas, the hormone *insulin* controls levels of glucose in the blood. Insulin was first isolated in 1921 by Canadian scientists Frederick Banting and Charles Best.

KIDNEYS
In 1842, British doctor William Bowman described the microscopic structure of the kidney. Two years later, in 1844, German scientist Karl Ludwig discovered how the kidneys make urine.

STOMACH
Digestion in the stomach was first described in 1833 by American doctor William Beaumont. He experimented by dangling food into a man's stomach through a hole in his side created by a shooting accident.

LIVER
In the 1850's, French physiologist Claude Bernard was the first person to investigate what the liver, the body's largest internal organ, does. We now know the liver performs over 500 vital functions.

BONE
Bones are hard and strong because they contain rigid, microscopic cylinders that lie in parallel to each other. These are named *Haversian systems* after Clopton Havers, a British doctor who described bone structure in 1691.

MUSCLES
How muscles contract to pull bones and move the body was discovered independently in 1954 by British scientists Andrew Huxley and Hugh Huxley.

MEDICINE

A disease or illness stops your body from working normally. The study of medicine involves finding out how a disease can be cured and prevented. Advances in medicine mean that today's doctors can diagnose and treat many illnesses. Hi-tech methods, such as CT scans, allow doctors to look inside a living body for possible problems. Drugs, such as the germ-killing antibiotic *penicillin*, are being developed all the time to combat specific diseases. Modern surgery removes, repairs, or replaces damaged body parts.

An 18th century case of surgical instruments. Many of the implements were used for amputations—a common remedy when little was know about bacterial infections.

• See page 15 THE STORY OF DNA
• See page 17 THE STORY OF GENETIC ENGINEERING

STETHOSCOPE

In 1819, French doctor René Laënnec invented the first stethoscope, an instrument used by doctors to listen to a patient's breathing and heart rate. Since 1819, Laënnec's *cylindre*, a wooden tube, has been improved upon many times to produce the instrument used today.

ANTISEPTIC SURGERY

Joseph Lister was a British surgeon and the founder of antiseptic surgery.

- In 1867, Lister introduced dressings soaked in carbolic acid and strict rules of hygiene to kill bacteria.

- Lister's methods increased the survival rate from surgery dramatically. Prior to this, around half of all surgical patients died from gangrene or secondary infections.

Joseph Lister

ALEXANDER FLEMING 1881–1955

Sir Alexander Fleming at a microscope in his laboratory at St. Mary's Hospital, London, c 1929.

Nationality: Scottish

Profession: Bacteriologist

Biographical information: Fleming trained as a doctor in London and served in the Medical Corps during World War I. He became interested in the problem of controlling infections caused by bacteria and continued his research after the war.

Eureka moment: One morning in 1928, Fleming was preparing a routine set of bacteria cultures when he noticed that something was killing the bacteria. When he investigated, he found that it was a bread mould, called *penicillin*.

Most famous discovery: Fleming discovered penicillin, the first antibiotic. Antibiotics are drugs that kill bacteria. They are now used to treat many illnesses and diseases.

Scientists at work: Two other scientists, Howard Florey and Ernst Chain, helped perfect the manufacture of penicillin, and they shared the 1945 Nobel Prize for medicine with Fleming.

DISCOVERING X-RAYS

WILHELM ROENTGEN

In November 1895, German physicist Wilhelm Roentgen found that by passing electricity through a vacuum he produced a new type of high energy radiation that he called *X-* (for *unknown*) *rays.*

An X-ray of Roentgen's wife's hand, 1895.

SEEING BONES

Roentgen also discovered that a beam of X-rays could pass through the body to produce an image on a photographic plate. Roentgen found that while bones appeared as clear images on the plate, soft tissues, such as muscle and skin, were much less distinct.

LOOKING INSIDE THE BODY

Within weeks, Roentgen's discovery was greeted as one of the most significant in the history of medicine. For the first time doctors could look inside the living body without having to cut it open. Today, X-rays are used routinely to detect broken bones and other disorders.

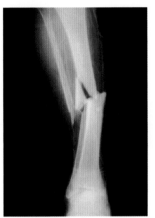

An X-ray showing a broken leg bone.

CT SCANNERS

X-rays are also used in combination with computers in computed tomography scanners. CT scanners produce images in the form of body "slices" that show both hard and soft tissues, an idea first developed by British engineer Godfrey Hounsfield in 1967.

TIMELINE: FIRST HEART TRANSPLANT

In December, 1967, South African surgeon Christiaan Barnard became the first person to perform a successful, human heart transplant.

Barnard draws a simple diagram of his pioneering procedure for reporters at a press conference following the ground-breaking surgery.

December 3, 1967
Christiaan Barnard leads a team of twenty surgeons in a revolutionary operation at the Groote Schuur Hospital, Cape Town, South Africa. Barnard replaces the heart of South African grocer, Louis Washkansky (who has an incurable heart disease) with a healthy heart from a fatally injured accident victim.

December 21, 1967
Washkansky dies from double pneumonia, but he has lived for 18 days with the donor heart and the operation is deemed a success.

1970s
Barnard's heart transplant operations are increasingly successful and by the late 1970s, a number of his patients have survived for several years.

SURGICAL TIMELINE

1770s – Art of surgery
English doctor John Hunter transforms surgery (the process of cutting into the body to treat disease) from a lowly craft to a progressive medical science.

1846 – Anaesthetic
The first public demonstration of ether anaesthetic is carried out by anaesthetist William Morton during a surgical operation in Boston, USA.

1865 – Antiseptic surgery
Joseph Lister pioneers use of germ-killing antiseptic during operations.

1937 – Hip replacement
In London, surgeon Philip Wiles performs the first hip replacement surgery using a stainless steel "ball and socket."

1940 – Plastic surgery
First skin grafts, to repair burns suffered by WWII pilots, carried out by English surgeon Archibald McIndoe.

1944 – Cardiac surgery
Pioneering operation by American doctors Alfred Blalock and Helen Taussig to treat heart disease in babies establishes specialty of cardiac (heart) surgery.

1954 – Kidney transplant
First successful kidney transplant operation (transferring a healthy kidney from a donor to a recipient with a diseased kidney) carried out in Boston, by Joseph Murray.

1967 – Heart transplant
First heart transplant operation carried out by South African surgeon Christiaan Barnard.

1969 – Microsurgery
First use, in USA, of microsurgery in which a surgeon uses a binocular microscope to magnify tiny blood vessels or nerves while repairing them.

1980 – Keyhole surgery
Introduction of "keyhole" surgery, *called laparoscopic-assisted surgery,* carried out through small incisions in the skin.

1987 – Laser eye surgery
In America, laser eye surgery using intense heat to repair damaged tissues first performed.

2002 – Surgical robots
First robot-assisted cardiac operation in the USA.

EDWARD JENNER 1749–1823

Nationality: British
Profession: Doctor
Biographical information: Edward Jenner trained as a surgeon before studying medicine in London. He returned home as a doctor in 1773.
Most famous discovery: The discovery and initial development of vaccination.

Eureka moment: Milkmaid Sarah Nelmes boasted that she could not catch smallpox because she had earlier caught the less serious disease cowpox from the cows she milked. A smallpox outbreak in 1788 proved that she was right. All of Jenner's patients who had caught cowpox did not get smallpox.

Scientist at work: Jenner proved his theory by infecting a small boy first with cowpox and then with smallpox. He found that the boy was immune to smallpox. Jenner called his treatment *vaccination* (from the Latin word for *cowpox, vaccina*).

• See page 35 for more info on fashion inventions.

EARLY INDUSTRY

The Industrial Revolution spread across three centuries and was the result of countless inventions, developments, and improvements. Two key factors were the widespread availability of metals, especially iron and steel, and the introduction of machinery. The textile industry was the first to be affected by the Industrial Revolution. The first modern factories were built in the 18th century for spinning cotton in northern England.

The Spinning Jenny

THE JACQUARD LOOM

- The first programmable machine was Joseph-Marie Jacquard's loom.

- The pattern woven by the loom was controlled by cards with holes punched in them. Changing the pattern of holes changed the pattern woven into the cloth.

MUNTZ METAL

In 1832, English businessman George Muntz invented an alloy of copper (60%) and zinc (40%), it was known as *Muntz metal.* This new alloy soon replaced pure copper for sheathing the hulls of wooden ships, making it stronger.

THE STORY OF MASS PRODUCTION

Mass production depends of three things: the use of machinery, interchangeable components, and the assembly line.

MADE BY HAND
The first machines are individually made by hand. The idea of interchangeable parts is first introduced in France, in 1785, for making the firing mechanisms of sporting guns.

MANUFACTURING FIREARMS
In 1801, inventor Eli Whitney demonstrates his system of interchangeable parts for the manufacture of military firearms.

SAMUEL COLT
In 1855, American industrialist Samuel Colt sets up a factory that uses interchangeable parts and a production line to make handguns of his own design.

RANSOM OLDS
In 1901, inventor Ransom Olds introduces production line methods into the newly established automobile industry for the manufacture of his Oldsmobile buggy, in the USA.

MODEL T PRODUCTION LINE
In 1913, American industrialist Henry Ford builds the world's first fully integrated factory assembly line for the production of the famous Model T Ford.

Workers add parts to cars as the cars move by. The man hours required to build a car go down from 12 hours to an hour and a half. A car is produced every 24 seconds.

• See page 26 HENRY FORD

A line of Model T chassis. The car bodies were manufactured on the upper floor of the factory, then lowered onto the chassis, which were built on the lower floor.

THE CONSTRUCTION INDUSTRY

FIRST IRON BRIDGE

In 1777, the world's first iron bridge is constructed across the River Severn at Coalbrookdale in Shropshire, England.

PRE-FABRICATED BUILDING

In 1851, The Crystal Palace is built entirely from iron and glass to accommodate the Great Exhibition in London, England. Engineer and botanist Joseph Paxton designs the building, based on the design of greenhouses used for growing plants. Paxton's revolutionary design contains over 300,000 panes of glass and hundreds of ready-made, cast-iron frames that simply bolt together on site.

REINFORCED CONCRETE

In 1867, in France, amateur inventor Joseph Monier makes the first successful reinforced concrete using lateral iron rods.

The Crystal Palace under construction.

IRON BUILDINGS

In 1889, the Eiffel Tower in Paris, France, is the last major building to be made from iron—in the future, steel will be used.

STEEL-FRAMED SKYSCRAPER

By the second half of the 19th century, business space in US cities is in great demand. The refinement of the Bessemer steel-making process in 1855 makes it possible to construct very high buildings, because steel is both stronger and lighter than iron. The development of the first safety lift also makes skyscrapers (buildings of 10 to 20 stories high) possible.

PRE-STRESSED CONCRETE

In 1928, French Engineer Eugene Freyssinet is the first to make use of prestressed concrete.

AN EXPLOSIVE INVENTION

DYNAMITE

The invention: Dynamite is a type of nitro-glycerine explosive that could be handled safely. Dynamite became used widely in the mining and construction industries.

Invented: 1866

Invented by: Swedish chemist Alfred Nobel

Other inventions: Blasting gelatin, smokeless powder for firearms, and explosives specifically for military purposes (although

Nobel later developed a bad conscience about this).

Inventor fact: When Nobel died in 1896, he bequeathed most of his fortune to establish Nobel Prizes for peace and scientific achievement.

OTIS SAFETY ELEVATOR

- Elisha Otis worked in a US bed factory. Simple cargo elevators were used to move goods to upper floors. Otis invented a safety device thathad arms that shot out from the elevator car and grabbed the side of the shaft if the rope broke. To demonstrate his invention, he had the cable cut while he was in a lift at the World's Fair of 1853.

- Skyscrapers would not have been built were it not for Otis's invention.

FANTASTIC PLASTIC

Plastics replaced traditional materials used in industry, such as wood, metal, glass, ceramics, natural fibers, ivory, and bone.

PARKESINE

In 1862, the English chemist Alexander Parkes produces the world's first plastic, named *Parkesine*. The material can be squeezed into a mold while soft and is made into small decorative items.

CELLULOID

During the late 1860s, American inventor John Hyatt discovers how to make celluloid while looking for an ivory substitute for making billiard balls. Celluloid is made into combs, piano keys, dolls, knife handles, and film. However, it is highly flammable and causes many accidents.

BAKELITE

In 1910, the Belgian-born American chemist Leo Baekeland invents the first thermosetting plastic, a plastic that sets permanently when heated. It is named *Bakelite*. Hard and chemically resistant, Bakelite is a nonconductor of electricity so it can be used in all sorts of electrical appliances.

POLYCARBONATE

In 1953, Dr. Daniel Fox, a chemist at General Electric, creates a gooey substance that hardens in a beaker. He finds he cannot break or destroy the material. LEXAN polycarbonate has been invented. Available in over 35,000 colors, polycarbonate has now been used in vehicle windows, helmets worn by the first astronauts on the moon, fighter jet windshields, laptop computer housings, CDs, and DVDs.

IRON & STEEL TIMELINE

1709 – QUALITY IRON

In England, Abraham Darby first produces good quality iron by smelting iron ore with baked coal. Baked coal burns with a hotter flame than charcoal and can be used to fuel much larger furnaces.

1709 – IRON BARS

In Sweden, the engineer Christopher Polhelm invents a grooved roller that can be used for making iron bars.

1750 – CRUCIBLE STEEL

In England, clockmaker Benjamin Huntsman perfects a process for making steel by heating high-quality iron in a special reverbatory furnace. Called *crucible steel*, this new metal is so hard to work with that knife makers at first refuse to use it.

1783 – PUDDLING PROCESS

The English ironmaker Henry Cort patents his "puddling" process that converts the brittle "pig iron," produced by smelting, into wrought iron which can be easily hammered and pressed into pots, pans and other household items.

1847 – STEEL MAKER

The American iron maker William Kelly discovers that he can convert iron to steel by blasting jets of air onto molten iron.

1855 – BESSEMER PROCESS

In England, the inventor Henry Bessemer patents his own method of making steel using blasts of air.

1864 – SIEMENS-MARTIN

The Martin iron works in France begins producing steel in an open-hearth furnace invented by the German engineer William Siemens. The Siemens-Martin process later becomes the world's leading method of steel production.

1866 – AIR BOILING

In the USA, Henry Kelly patents his "air boiling" method of steel making.

1877 – QUALITY STEEL

In England, cousins Percy and Sidney Gilchrist invent a method of dephosphorizing steel to produce better quality metal.

- **See page 12 DISCOVERING AND INVENTING METAL**

• See page 24
THE STORY OF MASS PRODUCTION

ENGINE POWER

For thousands of years, people had to rely on muscle power for making overland journeys. They walked, rode on horseback, or sat in a wagon pulled by animals to travel. Beginning in the 18th century, the traditional forms of transport were transformed by the invention and development of new sources of mechanical power in the form of the steam engine, and later, the internal combustion engine.

The blossoming film industry of the 1920s was quick to see the potential of the motor car—Ford's Model Ts were soon in the movies!

INVENTION OF THE ENGINE

An engine is a device for transforming heat from burned fuel into motive power.

INTERNAL OR EXTERNAL?
Steam engines are external combustion engines. The fuel is burned in a separate boiler, external from the engine, to make the steam that provides the force. Internal combustion engines, such as gas or diesel engines, burn their fuel inside the engine.

THE FOUR STROKE ENGINE
In 1876, German engineer Nickolaus Otto built the first four-stroke internal combustion engine. It burned a mixture of air and coal gas. Four-stroke engines get their name because the piston goes through a repetitive cycle of four up and down movements or strokes. Otto engines become widely used in European factories.

THE GASOLINE ENGINE
In Germany, in 1885, Gottleib Daimler invented the gas engine when he developed a carburetor, a device that allows a four-stroke engine to burn a mixture of air and gas. The advantage of gas is that it is much easier to store than coal gas.

THE DIESEL ENGINE
In 1893, German engineer Rudolf Diesel invented a four-stroke engine that burned a mixture of air and diesel oil.

Nickolaus Otto's four-stroke engine

HENRY FORD 1863–1947

Nationality: American

Profession: Engineer and businessman

Biographical information: Henry Ford left school at 15 and apprenticed as a machinist. Later, he set up a sawmill and engineering workshop on his father's farm. He built his first car in a workshop behind his home in Detroit in 1896. In 1903, He set up the Ford Motor Company.

Most famous invention: In 1913, Ford invented the assembly line, an effcient way of making cars. The car moves along a track in the factory, and each worker adds one part to the car as it passes them.

Eureka moment: Ford realized that if he could produce cars cheaply enough, he could sell them in huge numbers and make big profits.

Henry Ford

BLACK GOLD

- In 1859, Edwin Drake drilled the world's first oil well in Pennsylvania. He struck oil 69.5 feet below the surface.

Edwin Drake (right) in 1866 with the first US oil well.

- At first, oil refineries concentrated on producing lubricating oils and paraffin for lamps. But after 1900, with the development of the internal combustion engine, gas and diesel fuel quickly became the most important refinery products.

SUPER STEAM

THE MALLARD

The fastest steam locomotive ever was the *Mallard*. It achieved a maximum speed of 126 mph in England in 1938. It was built by the British engineer Sir Nigel Gresley.

STEAM POWER

Cugnot's steam-powered tricycle had a top speed of 2 mph.

At first, steam power was mostly used to run stationary machines. It was only through the vision and determination of engineers and inventors that steam was eventually used to power the railways.

1698 - STEAM PUMP

In England, engineer Thomas Savery invents a pump that uses condensed steam to create a vacuum that draws water up a pipe. The machine is used to pump water from underground mines.

1712 - BEAM ENGINE

English engineer Thomas Newcomen invents the first true steam engine. It uses a pair of pistons in cylinders to tilt the ends of a centrally positioned horizontal beam that operates a pump.

1769 - STEAM WAGON

French army engineer Nicholas Cugnot builds the world's first steam-powered land vehicle. Cugnot's prototype three-wheeled artillery tractor can pull loads of up to 3-tons. However, the weight of the huge copper boiler at the front makes it difficult to steer. On its first trip, it runs into a wall.

1791 - ROTARY POWER

Scottish engineer James Watt perfects a steam engine that is capable of powering other machines. Watt's machine has a flywheel, which converts the up and down movement of a piston into rotary motion.

1801-1808 RAILWAY LOCOMOTIVES

Richard Trevithick builds a steam locomotive for an ironworks in Coalbrookdale, in Shropshire, England. In 1808, he gives rides to passengers around a circular track built in London in his "Catch Me Who Can" steam train.

1807 - STEAMBOAT SERVICE

In the USA, the engineer Robert Fulton starts a steamboat service on the Hudson River between the cities of New York and Albany. The service is reliable and successful.

1830 - ROCKET

A 31-mile railway line between the cities of Liverpool and Manchester in England is built primarily to carry passengers. A locomotive named the *Rocket*, designed by the engineer Robert Stephenson, pulls the first train in 1930. For a short stretch Rocket reaches 36 mph.

The Stephenson's Rocket locomotive sits next to a larger, more modern British steam locomotive.

FASTEST ON FOUR WHEELS

1899 – 100 km/h barrier
The French engineer Camille Jenatzy builds an electric car that becomes the first vehicle to break the 100 km/h barrier (62.2 mph).

1906 – Stanley steamer
A *Stanley Steamer* built by the American brothers Francis and Freelan Stanley reaches a road speed of 127.4 mph.

1921 – 208 mph
French driver Sadi Lecointe reaches 208 mph in a gas-engine Nieuport-Delage racing car.

1988 – Solar power
In the USA, driver Molly Brennan achieves a top speed of 48.71 mph in a solar-powered vehicle called *Sunraycer*.

1997 – Sound barrier
In the Black Rock Desert, Nevada, Andy Green breaks the sound barrier in *Thrust SSC*, reaching a speed of 763 mph.

ON THE ROAD TIMELINE

1952 – Airbag
First patented in 1952 by American John W. Hetrick, and with a practical version developed in 1973, airbags were fitted to most cars in the US by 1988, and later to European cars.

1959 – Seat belt
First fitted to a 1959 Volvo, Nils Bohlin's "lap-and-diagonal" design seat belts anchor passengers to the car. Seat belts have since prevented millions of injuries.

1954 – Breathalyzer
Robert Borkenstein, a police officer in Indiana, invented the breathalyzer. It uses chemicals that turn from orange to green, indicating the amount of alcohol in the breath.

• See page 52 A–Z INVENTIONS for more travel-related inventions.

1485 – Flapping design
Italian artist and inventor Leonardo da Vinci sketches a man-powered aircraft made of wood and fabric. Da Vinci's design is intended to imitate the flight of birds with flapping wings.

1804 – Fixed wings
In England, amateur flight enthusiast and inventor George Caley builds a model fixed-wing glider that establishes the basic configuration of the modern aircraft. The glider was strong enough to carry a boy, and a later, stronger model carries Caley's coachman across a narrow valley.

1896 – Hang glider
In Germany, inventor Otto Lilienthal is killed after crashing into the ground while testing his latest design for a hang-glider. Previously Lilienthal had successfully "flown" distances of more than 1150 feet and had made more than 2,500 flights.

1903 – Powered flight
Orville and Wilbur Wright achieve the world's first powered flight.

1907 – First helicopter
French mechanic Paul Cornu becomes the first person to build and fly a helicopter. It hovers just off the ground for 20 seconds. Then, the fuselage rotates in the opposite direction to the rotor blades causing the machine to crash to the ground.

1909 – Cross-channel
French engineer and aviator Louis Bleriot makes the first flight across the English Channel in the *Type XI* monoplane that he designed and built.

1919 – First across ocean
Setting off from Newfoundland and landing in Ireland, English pilots John Alcock and Arthur Brown fly a *Vickers Vimy* biplane across the Atlantic Ocean. The engines get blocked by ice several times while flying, and Brown has to climb along the wings to chip away the ice with a knife.

- The TIMELINE continues on page 29.

PLANES AND BOATS

Until the invention of powered flight, the only way to cross seas and oceans was by ship. Early sailors in wooden sailing ships were constantly at the mercy of the winds and high seas. In the 19th century, technological innovations, such as iron hulls and steam engines, made shipping faster, safer, and more reliable. Since the beginning of the 20th century, the development of aircraft has shrunk long-distance journey times from weeks to a matter of hours.

THE FIRST FLIGHT

- December 17, 1903, Wilbur and Orville Wright travel to the sand dunes outside Kitty Hawk in North Carolina, with their plane, *Flyer*.

- Only five people witness the world's first powered flight.

- Wilbur runs alongside Flyer holding one wing to balance the plane on the track.

- Orville operates the controls lying face down on the lower wing.

- The flight lasts 12 seconds and covers a distance of 120 feet. The brothers make three more successful flights that day.

ORVILLE AND WILBUR WRIGHT

Wilbur: 1867–1912
Orville: 1871–1948

Nationality: American

Profession: Engineers

Biographical information: Orville and Wilbur Wright were brothers. From an early age, they were interested in engineering. They owned a business manufacturing and designing bicycles.

Eureka moment: In 1899, Wilbur, while watching birds, realized that an airplane must be able to bank to one side or another, to climb or descend, and to steer left or right.

Most famous invention: The airplane—they demonstrated the first powered, controlled, and sustained flight in their plane, *Flyer*.

Inventors at work: The Wright brothers built gliders to perfect the controls for their plane, a lightweight petrol engine to power it and an efficient propeller. They even built a wind tunnel to aid their experiments. The brothers approach to inventing was scientific—they thought about a machine's requirements in advance, rather than "building the machine and seeing what happened," like their aviation predecessors had.

Flyer at Kitty Hawk

INVENTING THE JET ENGINE

INVENTION OF THE JET ENGINE
In 1930, Royal Air Force pilot Frank Whittle patents his idea for the jet engine, an aircraft engine that uses a jet of heated air to produce thrust. Whittle recognizes the potential for an aircraft that can fly at high speeds. He proves mathematically that his invention can work, but the Air Ministry is not interested.

THE FIRST JET ENGINE
Whittle builds his jet engine and on April 12, 1937, the turbojet engine has its maiden run on the ground. With the outbreak of WWII, the British Government now back Whittle, but it is German inventors who develop the first operational jet aircraft in 1939.

Whittle's engine

TEST PILOTS

Test pilots make aircraft inventions possible. They put new designs of air and spacecraft through manoeuvres designed to test the machines' capabilities. In 1947, the sound barrier was broken for the first time. American test pilot Chuck Yeager flew the air-launched, rocket-powered *Bell X-1* aircraft. *The X-1* reached 700 mph at an altitude of 43,000 feet.

THE BALLOON INVENTERS

1783 - FIRST HUMAN FLIGHT

The first humans ever to fly a hot air balloon invented and built by French brothers Jacques and Joseph Montgolfier.

• See page 48 for more information on JACQUES AND JOSEPH MONTGOLFIER

1783 - HYDROGEN BALLOON

Shortly after the Montgolfier's hot-air balloon flight, the French scientist Jacques Alexandre César Charles makes the first flight in a balloon containing lighter-than-air hydrogen gas. Charles's balloon travels about 29 miles.

1900 - ZEPPELINS

In Germany, LZ-1, the first large airship designed by the engineer Ferdinand von Zeppelin, successfully takes to the air. Subsequently, zeppelins are used both for warfare, as bombers, and for carrying passengers. In 1937, the Hindenburg airship disaster brings the airship era to an abrupt end.

1932 - AUGUSTE PICARD

Professor Auguste Picard takes his hot-air balloon to a height of 53,152 feet. Picard risks burst blood

vessels and eardrums, and even black-outs because his capsule is not pressurized as modern aircraft are today.

1961 - RECORD-BREAKER

A US Navy research helium balloon carries two pilots, Malcolm Ross and Vic Parther, to an altitude of 113,740 feet above the Earth's surface.

1999 - CIRCUMNAVIGATION

Balloon enthusiasts Bertrand Piccard and Brian Jones circumnavigate the world (25,361 miles) in Breitling Orbiter 3. The helium balloon uses air currents to control its course. Orbiter 3 is 780 feet high and can contain the contents of seven olympic-sized swimming pools!

Piccard (right) and Jones operated *Breitling Orbiter 3* from this pressurized capsule that resembles a spacecraft.

THE FIRST SUBMARINE

The first submarine was a wooden rowing boat with a watertight cover of greased leather. It was designed in 1620 by Dutch engineer Cornelius van Drebbel.

The craft was powered by 12 oarsmen and reached depths of nearly 15 feet during tests on the Thames River in England. Passengers breathed through tubes that ran from the submarine to the surface of the water.

SHIP INNOVATIONS

1783

French engineers demonstrate that a steam engine can be used to propel a 165-ton riverboat.

1786

American engineer John Fitch designs and launches the world's first purpose-built steamboat on the Delaware River near Philadelphia.

1838

Swedish engineer John Ericsson uses his ship Archimedes to demonstrate that a steam-driven screw (propeller) is more efficient than a steam-driven paddlewheel

1797

The first ship with a completely metal hull (a 69-foot iron barge) is launched in England.

INVENTION OF THE HOVERCRAFT

- In 1955, British engineer Christopher Cockerell patented the hovercraft, a vehicle that moves on a cushion of air.

- In 1958, his prototype SR.N1 crossed the English Channel (34 kilometres) in 20 minutes.

- Cockerell patented around 70 inventions during his lifetime.

SR.N1 arrives at Dover after the first Channel crossing.

LONGITUDE

In the 18th century, sailors could tell their latitude (position north to south) from the position of the Sun. Longitude (position east to west) was difficult.

Comparing the time at home (using a clock onboard ship) with the time at sea, according to the position of the Sun, was feasible, but no pendulum clock could keep accurate time with the rolling of the sea.

In 1761, after several years work and four attempts, English clockmaker John Harrison invented a chronometer (a large watch-like clock) with a mechanism and dials. Harrison's invention kept such accurate time that a navigator could work out on a map where he was with an accuracy of less than a mile.

John Harrison's H4 watch.

AIRCRAFT TIMELINE

1927 – Solo Trans-Atlantic

American aviator Charles Lindberg makes the first solo flight across the Atlantic Ocean (from New York to Paris) in the Spirit of St. Louis, a single-engine M62.

1930 – Jet engine

In England, Royal Air Force pilot Frank Whittle patents his idea for a jet engine.

1939 – Jet aircraft

In Germany, the He 178 monoplane, designed by Ernst Heinkel, makes its first flight powered by a jet engine developed by engineer Pabst von Ohain.

1941 – Sikorsky helicopter

Russian-born aviator, Igor Sikorsky solves the problem of torque by fitting a small rotor on the tail of a helicopter. His VS300 hovers in the air for 102 minutes.

1952 – Jet Airliner

The world's first jet airliner, the de Havilland Comet, comes into service, carrying passengers between London, England and Johannesburg, South Africa.

1970 – Jumbo Jet

The first Boeing 747 Jumbo Jet airliner comes into service between New York and London. The jumbo jet can carry more than 360 passengers at a time.

1979 – Human-powered

American pilot Bryan Allen achieves the first human-powered cross-channel flight flying the pedal-powered Gossamer Albatross.

1986 – Around the world

American pilots Richard Rutan and Jeana Yeager fly nonstop around the world in the experimental Voyager aircraft. The flight, which lasts nine days, is made without refuelling.

2005 – Around the world again

Steve Fosset flies solo, nonstop around the world in 67 hours, 1 minute, and 46 seconds.

TELEGRAPH & TELEPHONE TIMELINE

1794 – Chappe's telegraph
Claude Chappe begins the construction of his telegraph across France.

1825 – Electro-magnet
The electro-magnet is invented. This is vital for the later invention of the telegraph.

1837 – Five-needle telegraph
William Fothergill Cooke and Charles Wheatstone invent the five-needle telegraph. It works by sending an electric current along wires that move two of the five needles, either left or right, so that they both point to one letter at a time.

1842 – Fax machine
The fax machine is invented by Alexander Bain, a physicist.

1843 – Morse telegraph
Morse demonstrates his telegraph to the American Congress, and they give him $30,000 to build a telegraph line from Washington D.C. to Baltimore, a distance of 40 miles.

1844 – Morse's message
Morse sends the first message on the new telegraph line. It reads, "What hath God Wrought."

1858 – Atlantic cable
A cable is laid between America and Britain so that telegraphs can be sent across the Atlantic. The cable fails within a month.

1860 – First telephone
German teacher Philipp Reis invents a simple telephone. Reis builds just 12 telephones before he dies. One of Reis's telephones reaches a student at Edinburgh University. That student student is Alexander Graham Bell.

•The TIMELINE continues on page 31.

When the American colonies declared their independence in 1776, it took 48 days for the news to cross the Atlantic. The arrival of the telegraph in 1843 and the telephone in 1876 meant that news could get to anywhere in the world almost instantly. The beginning of radio communication in 1896 meant that sounds could travel vast distances without the need for cables. When television arrived in 1936, moving pictures and sounds had the capability to be seen by millions at the same time anywhere in the world.

Wheatstone and Cooke's five-needle telegraph.

CHAPPE'S TELEGRAPH

- In 1793, France was at war. A quick way to warn of an invasion was needed. In 1794, Claude Chappe invented the telegraph.

- Chappe's telegraph used two arms at the top of a tall tower. Ropes and pulleys moved the arms into different positions each representing a letter.

- The towers were positioned 6 to 20 feet apart, and the messages were read by people using telescopes.

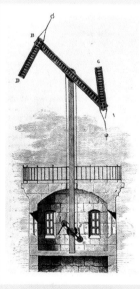

The main pole of the telegraph was about 20 feet tall.

MORSE CODE

- Samuel Morse invented Morse code in 1838. He first got the idea for the code in 1832 when he was told about experiments with electricity.

- Morse's idea was to develop a code based on interrupting the flow of electricity so that a message could be heard.

- Morse code works very simply. Electricity is either switched on or off. When it is on, it travels along a wire. The other end of the wire the electric current can either make a sound or be printed out.

- A short electric current, a *dit*, is printed as a dot and a longer *dah* is printed as a dash.

A	•–	N	–•
B	–•••	O	–––
C	–•–•	P	•––•
D	–••	Q	––•–
E	•	R	•–•
F	••–•	S	•••
G	––•	T	–
H	••••	U	••–
I	••	V	•••–
J	•–––	W	•––
K	–•–	X	–••–
L	•–••	Y	–•––
M	––	Z	––••

The full Morse code is based on combining dots and dashes to represent the letters of the alphabet.

• See page 48
SAMUEL MORSE

THE INVENTION OF THE POSTAGE STAMP

- In the early 1800s, postage in Britain was charged by distance and the number of sheets in a letter. The recipient paid for the postage not the sender.

- In 1837, retired English schoolteacher Rowland Hill wrote a pamphlet calling for cheap, standard postage rates, regardless of distance.

- The British Post Office took up Hill's ideas, and, in May 1840, issued the first adhesive postage stamps.

- The stamps were printed with black ink and become known as *Penny Blacks*.

ALEXANDER GRAHAM BELL 1847 – 1922

Nationality: Scottish-born American

Profession: Teacher and inventor

Biographical information: Bell left school at 14 and trained in the family business of teaching elocution (public speaking). His family moved to Canada in 1870. He trained people in his father's system of teaching deaf people to speak.

Most famous inventon: Working at night with his assistant, Thomas Watson, he made the first working telephone in 1876.

Inventors at work: The telegraph already used electricity to convey messages over long distances. The telephone had to turn sound into electricity and back again. Making it work was a challenge, which Bell and Watson solved by hard work over many months.

Eureka moment: The first words spoken on a telephone were, "Mr. Watson, come here, I want you!" Bell was testing out his newly invented telephone when he spilt some chemicals on his clothes and called to his assistant for help.

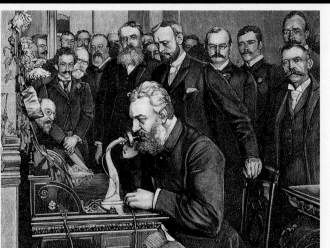

Alexander Graham Bell opens the New York to Chicago telephone line in 1892.

Bell experimented for many years with different ways of sending and receiving spoken messages. This Gallows Frame transmitter was one of his earliest machines.

THE INVENTION OF DIRECT DIALING

- At first, telephone connections were made by operators pushing plugs into sockets.

- In 1889, in Kansas City, undertaker Almon Strowger discovered that his local operator was married to a rival undertaker and was diverting his calls to her husband.

- Strowger invented the first automatic telephone switch. The remote-controlled switch that could connect one phone to any of several others by electrical pulses.

MOBILE PHONES AND TEXT MESSAGING

1973 – First mobile call
The first call made on a mobile phone is made in April by Dr. Martin Cooper, general manager of Motorola. He calls his rival, Joel Engel, the head of research at Bell Laboratories.

1992 – First text
The first text message is sent. It is reported that the message, "Merry Christmas," was from Neil Papworth of Vodaphone.

2000 – Camera phone
The camera phone is created by

Sharp in Japan. It is called the *J-Sh04*.

August 2001
The first month that over one billion text messages are sent by mobile phone.

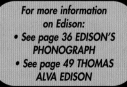

VIDEO PHONES

- The first videotelephone with a screen for moving pictures was invented by AT&T in 1964. It allowed people to look at the people they were calling.

- Using mobile phones to record videos started with the creation of 3G mobile phones by Dr. Irwin Jacobs in 2003.

TELEGRAPH & TELEPHONE TIMELINE

1861 – The pantelgraph
The first fax machine is sold. It is called the *Pantelgraph*.

Telegraphs can be sent from one end of America to the other.

1865 – Public fax
The first public fax service opens in France, used to send photographs to newspapers.

1866 – Atlantic cable
The ship, the *Great Eastern*, lays a second cable along the Atlantic seafloor.

1876 – Bell's telephone
Alexander Graham Bell invents the first successful telephone.

1878 – Thomas Edison
American inventor Thomas Edison has also been working on a telephone, but Bell beats him to it. Edison invents a microphone that makes the voice of the person speaking much clearer to the listener.

1880 – First pay phone
The first pay-phones opened in New York.

There are now nine separate cables between America and Britain.

1892 – Direct-dial
The first direct-dial telephones become operational.

1915 – First Atlantic call
First telephone calls across the Atlantic.

1936 – COAXIAL CABLE
The first coaxial cable is laid. This allows many telephone messages to pass along the same cable.

1963 – 160 MILLION
The number of telephones in the world reaches 160 million.

1988 – FIBER-OPTIC CABLE
The first fiber-optic cable is laid across the Atlantic. Now, telephone messages are carried on pulses of light.

For more information on Edison:
- *See page 36 EDISON'S PHONOGRAPH*
- *See page 49 THOMAS ALVA EDISON*

COMMUNICATIONS

RADIO TIMELINE

1873 — Electromagnetic waves
Scottish scientist James Clark Maxwell writes a paper about electromagnetic waves that can travel through the air. He could not prove they existed.

1887 — Heinrich Hertz
German scientist Heinrich Hertz transmits a spark using a tuned antenna. He also proves James Clark Maxwell's theory about the existence of radio waves, which are one kind of electromagnetic wave. However, the radio waves he created could not travel very far.

1894 — Marconi's bell
Marconi makes a bell ring using radio waves.

1897 — Shore to ship
Marconi transmits a signal from land to a ship eighteen miles out at sea. The British Royal Navy shows a great interest in this new invention.

1901 — Atlantic signal
Marconi sends a radio signal across the Atlantic Ocean.

1906 - Triode valve
The triode valve is invented by Lee DeForrest. It makes radio signals more powerful.

1906 — First voice and music
American scientist Reginald A. Fessenden transmits his voice and broadcasts music using radio waves. Before this, only morse code could be carried on radio waves. Following his groundbreaking achievement, Fessenden did not pursue his radio experiments.

1920 — First radio station
The world's first ever commercially licensed radio station, KDKA in Philadelphia, makes its first broadcast on November 2.

1923 — Atlantic voice
The first ever broadcast of a voice across the Atlantic Ocean is from Pittsburgh to Manchester, UK.

1947 — Transistor
The transistor is invented by engineers at Bell Laboratories.

1995 — Digital radio
BBC radio stations, in the UK, begin digital broadcasting.

GUGLIELMO MARCONI 1874–1937

Marconi, in 1896, with an early apparatus.

Nationality: Italian

Profession: Physicist

Biographical information: Marconi attended Technical College in Italy, where he studied electricity and magnetism. After leaving college, he continued his experiments at the family farm but could find little support for his work in Italy. In 1896, he moved to England.

Most famous invention: Marconi invented the first practical system of wireless communication using radio waves. In 1896, before leaving Italy, Marconi managed to transmit a radio signal over a distance of about one and a half kilometres. In England he quickly increased the range to about 62 miles, and in 1899, made radio contact between Britain and France.

Eureka moment: In 1901, Marconi successfully sent a radio message across the Atlantic Ocean, from Cornwall, England to St.John's, Canada, a distance of more than 2,500 miles.

Inventor at work: Marconi was awarded the 1909 Nobel Prize for physics. He continued to make numerous improvements to radio transmitting and receiving equipment.

CLOCKWORK RADIO

- In 1991, British inventor Trevor Baylis invented the wind-up radio, enabling millions in the developing world, with no permanent electricity supply, to receive broadcasts.

- The radio works by winding up a spring, which slowly uncoils and powers a small generator.

Inventor Trevor Baylis with his clockwork radio.

RADIO ON THE MOVE

Invented in 1947, the transistor replaced the valves inside radios that picked up radio signals. Transistors were much smaller than valves, so it now became possible to make portable radios.

October 18, 1954
The world's "first pocket radio" goes on sale. The *Regency TR1* is 5 inches high. About 100,000 *TR1*s are sold during the radio's first year of production.

1955
A Japanese company called *Tokyo Tsushin Kogyo* build a portable radio for the US market. In 1958, before they begin selling the radio, they change the company name to *Sony*.

A 1962 Sony transistor radio with wind up watch and alarm.

JOHN LOGIE BAIRD 1888-1946

Nationality: Scottish

Profession: Electrical engineer

Biographical information: Baird studied at the University of Glasgow where he first became interested in the idea of using radio waves to transmit pictures. At the time, most scientists considered such a system to be impossible.

Eureka moment: Baird realized that pictures could be sent by radio if the images were broken down into a series of electronic impulses. He invented a mechanical scanner that, by 1926, was able to scan and transmit moving images.

Most famous invention: In 1926, using equipment that he had made himself, Baird demonstrated the world's first working television system.

Other inventions: Baird also demonstrated color television in 1928 and continued to work researching stereoscopic television.

In 1936, he demonstrated his mechanical system to the BBC, but they chose an electronic system from EMI.

Televisor screen

The televisor, a mechanical television set invented by Baird. Viewers watched the first television broadcasts on these sets.

SATELLITES

Much of our long-distance communication relies on the hundreds of satellites that are in orbit around the Earth.

- Each satellite receives a radio or television signal from one place and then transmits it onwards.

- Most of the satellites are geostationary, which means they are traveling at the same speed as the Earth's rotation and will always be at the same point in the sky.

- In summer 1962, the USA launched the *Telstar* satellite.

- Telstar provided a radio and television link between Europe and America for just a few hours every day.

Telstar

THE ELECTRONIC PIONEERS

Vladimir Zworykin, vice president of RCA, c 1951

Baird is credited with the invention of television, but the systems we use and the TVs we watch today owe much to earlier inventors (see timeline, right) and to two pioneers of the electronic television, Zworykin and Shoenberg.

Vladimir Zworykin
- Russian born Vladimir Zworykin emigrated to the USA in 1919.

- Zworykin was the first to take up the suggestion by Scottish engineer Alan Campbell Swinton that it should be possible to both create and display pictures using a cathode ray tube.

- In 1931, heading a team at RCA, Zworykin created the first successful electronic camera tube, the iconoscope.

Isaac Shoenberg
- Russian-born Isaac Shoenberg also emigrated to Britain in 1914.

- In 1936, working with a team at Electrical and Musical Industries (EMI), Schoenberg used Zworykin's basic idea to develop the Emitron tube which formed the heart of the cameras demonstrated for the BBC.

The winning system
In 1936, EMI's all electronic system was demonstrated to the BBC and was chosen over the mechanical system demonstrated by Baird. Except for some specific differences, the EMI system is the one in use today.

TELEVISION TIMELINE

1860s – Pantelegraph
The Italian physicist, Abbe Giovanni Caselli, sends images over a long distance, using a system he calls the *pantelegraph*. Caselli's system is the first prototype of a fax machine.

1873 – Pictures into signals
Two British telegraph engineers, May and Smith, find a way of turning pictures into electrical signals.

1884 – Mechanical TV
German engineer Paul Nipkow discovers television's scanning principle. His invention, a rotating disc with spirals of apertures that pass successively across the picture, will make a mechanical television system possible.

1897 – Cathode ray tube
Karl Ferdinand Braun, a German physicist, invents the first cathode ray tube. This is used in modern television cameras and TV sets.

1906 – 1907
Boris Rosing of Russia develops a system combining the cathode ray with a Nipkow disc, creating the world's first working television system. In 1907, Rosing transmits black and white silhouettes of simple shapes.

1924 – First moving image
The Scottish engineer John Logie Baird is the first to transmit a moving image, using a system based on Nipkow's disc.

1925 – First face on TV
Baird transmits recognizable human faces.

1926 – Moving objects
Baird demonstrates the televising of moving objects at the Royal Institute.

1936 – BBC
The BBC (British Broadcasting Corporation) starts the world's first public television service in London.

1951 – Color TV
The first color television transmissions begin in the USA.

1989 – Satellite TV
The first satellite television stations are launched with four channels.

1998 – Digital TV
First digital satellite television stations launched.

1740 – Franklin stove
American Benjamin Franklin invents a simple, cast-iron stove, similar to modern-day woodburners, for warming homes.

1792 – Gas lighting
In 1792, Scottish engineer William Murdock invents gas lighting. He heats coal in a closed vessel and then pumps the gas to lights around his cottage in Cornwall, England.

1830 – Lawnmower
Patented in 1830, Edwin Budding's cylinder lawnmower makes lawns available to all homes. Before this, only people with a gardener or flock of sheep could maintain a lawn.

1844 - Refrigerator
American doctor John Gorrie builds a machine that uses compressed air to provide cooling air for feverish patients in his hospital. In 1851, he receives the first US patent for mechanical refrigeration.

c 1860 – Linoleum
British rubber manufacturer Frederick Walton invents linoleum, a washable floor covering made from cloth covered with a linseed oil and pine resin substance.

1907 – Washing machine
US inventor Alva Fisher invents the first electric washing machine. The machine has a drum that tumbles the clothes and water backward and forward. The machine is called the Thor.

1919 – Pop-up toaster
US inventor Charles Strite invents the first toaster to automatically stop toasting and pop out the toast when it is ready. It will be nine years before Otto Rohwedder invents sliced bread.

1946 – Microwave oven
In 1945, US engineer Percy LeBaron Spencer invents the microwave oven. While working on radar, Spencer makes the discovery that powerful microwaves had melted some chocolate in his pocket.

• See page 44
DOMESTIC ROBOTS

HOME AND FASHION

While most home and fashion-related inventions could not claim to have changed our world, they have certainly made it more colorful, comfortable, and clean. Today, we wear clothes and shoes made from a variety of different materials. We take it for granted that electric lights will illuminate our homes, that chilled food and drinks will stay that way in the refrigerator, and that the toilet will flush.

THE INVENTION OF THE *DYSON*

- In 1978, British inventor James Dyson noticed that the dust bag in conventional vacuum cleaners quickly clogged up.

- Dyson had the idea of making a bagless cleaner. It used centrifugal force to suck dust into a plastic cylinder.

- Five years and 5,127 prototypes later, Dyson was finally making and marketing a vacuum cleaner called the *Dyson Dual Cyclone*. The *Cyclone* was first real breakthrough since the vacuum cleaner's invention in 1901.

The Dyson DC15

• See page 56
VACUUM CLEANER

TOILET INVENTIONS

FIRST FLUSHING TOILET

- Sir John Harington was a British writer. His godmother was Queen Elizabeth I.

- In 1596, he published a humorous work entitled *The Metamorphosis of Ajax* (a play on the word *jakes*, slang for *lavatory*). It included diagrams of a flushing toilet, or water closet.

- Harrington's toilet design had a bowl, a seat, and a cistern of water for washing away the toilet's contents.

- Harrington built just two of his toilets, one for himself and one for the queen at Richmond Palace.

THOMAS CRAPPER

- In the 1800s, toilet pioneers, such as Thomas Crapper, began to develop the toilet further and produce the items we recognize today.

- Crapper registered a number of patents, including a spring-loaded toilet seat that lifted as soon as the user stood and pulling rods that automatically flushed the pan.

TOILET PAPER

- American Joseph Gayetty is credited with inventing toilet paper in 1857. Before Gayetty's invention, people tore pages out of mail order cataloges.

- In 1880, the British Perforated Paper Company invented a type of toilet paper. The shiny paper came in small sheets in a box.

THE LIGHT BULB

- Working independently, Sir Joseph Wilson Swan and Thomas Edison each invented a light bulb.

- Swan, a British inventor, is best known for his incandescent-filament electric lamp of 1879. It gave off light as an electric current passed through its carbon filament contained in a glass bulb.

- In America, Edison had the same idea. By 1880, he and Swan had developed efficient, long-lasting, light bulbs. In 1883, they formed the Edison & Swan Electric Light Company.

THE INVENTION OF JEANS

The invention of jeans is basically the story of *Levi's® 501® Jeans.*

- Levi Strauss ran the San Francisco branch of his brothers' dry goods business and supplied cloth to Jacob Davis, a tailor.

- To cure the problem of his customers ripping their work pants, Jacob came up with the idea of using metal rivets to strengthen the points of strain. This was a great success.

- Needing money to patent his invention, Jacob teamed up with Levi. On May 20, 1873, the two men received patent no.139,121 from the US Patent Office. Blue jeans were born.

- Around 1890, the *waist overalls*, as they were called, were assigned the number *501.*

- The word *jeans* was coined around 1960.

Vintage Levi 501s

THE INVENTION OF ATHLETIC SHOES

The adidas® Hyperride

Adolf (Adi) Dassler made his first shoes in 1920. He was just 20 years old. Dassler's vision was to provide every athlete with the best footwear for his or her discipline.

- Athletes wore special shoes from his workshop for the first time at the 1928 Olympic Games held in Amsterdam.

- By the mid 1930s, Dassler was making 30 different shoes for 11 sports, and his company was the world's leading sports shoe manufacturer.

- In 1948, he introduced *adidas* (a combination of his names) as the company name, and a year later he registered the unmistakable 'Three Stripes'.

- In 1954, when Germany won the World Cup in soccer, the team were wearing shoes with screw-in studs, made by adidas.

Adi Dassler in his sports shoes factory.

BABY FASHION

US engineer Vic Mills did not like the cloth diapers worn by his grandaughter, so he challenged the US company Procter & Gamble to find a solution to the problem.

In 1961, after years of testing, diapers called *Pampers®* were sold.

THE INVENTION OF NYLON

While a professor at Harvard University in 1928, Wallace Carothers was hired by the chemical company DuPont. Carothers' mission was to, "Get rid of the worms!"

1928 - A SILK SUBSTITUTE
Dupont wanted Carothers to make a substitute for silk, the fine and very costly fiber that is spun by silkworms.

Carothers set to work with a team of eight people, including scientist Julian Hill.

1930 - INVENTING PLASTICS
The team's first breakthrough was neoprene, and soon after, a plastic called *3-16 polymer.*

When Hill dipped a rod into *3-16*, he could pull out a thread. The more he stretched the thread, the stronger it became.

The threads were springy as silk, could be made from oil, water, and air and no silkworms were required.

1934 - NYLON
The *3-16* polymer was not suitable for cloth production, since ironing melted it, but by tweaking the recipe they produced the "artificial silk" required. Five more years of research and the newly-named *nylon* was ready to go.

GORE-TEX

In 1969, American inventor Bob Gore discovered that a new material could be produced from the polymer polytetrafluoroethylene (PTFE).

He invented GORE-TEX, the world's first completely waterproof, windproof and breathable fabric. Many other fabrics could repel water, but they did not breathe, so the wearer still got wet inside their clothing from the moisture produced by their own body.

GORE-TEX has now been worn by Antarctic explorers and even space shuttle astronauts!

THE MACKINTOSH

In 1823, the Scottish chemist Charles Macintosh invented a method of using rubber to produce waterproof cloth.

His name (misspelled as *mackintosh* or shortened to *mac*) becomes the popular name for a raincoat. They are known as *slickers* in the US.

• See page 49
THOMAS ALVA EDISON

In the past, hobbies were limited by the amount of free time available to people. Toys were primarily simple adaptations of everyday items. Now, people have much leisure time and spending power. For the past 150 years, inventors and innovators have used their talents to entertain us and satisfy our demands, from simple toys like building blocks, to the latest equipment for downloading music.

Edison's phonograph, the first sound recording machine

MUSICAL INVENTIONS

c 1700 – Clarinet
The German musician and instrument maker Johann Denner develops the clarinet from an earlier musical instrument, called the *chalumeau*.

1709 – Piano
Italian harpsichord builder Bartolomeo Cristofori invents a touch-sensitive harpsichord. This new instrument will eventually become the piano. Harpsichords plucked their strings, but Cristofori's new instrument hits the strings with hammers, so the harder the keyboard was struck, the louder it played.

1948 – Long-playing record
Engineer Peter Goldmark develops a vinyl disc for Columbia Records that can play 25 minutes of sound each side.

1949 – 45rpm single
RCA Victor brings out the *single*, a 7 inch record that holds one song on each side at a spead of 45 rotations per minute.

EDISON'S PHONOGRAPH

• Shouting into the horn of Edison's phonograph (see above) made a needle vibrate and scratch a groove into tin-foil wrapped around a spinning cylinder.

• When the needle was moved back to the beginning of the cylinder, the groove made the needle vibrate.

• The tiny vibrations were made loud enough to hear by the machine's horn, recreating the original sound.

THE WALKMAN

• In 1979, Sony engineers took just four days to create a prototype, pocket-sized tape player with earphones, an idea devised by Masura Ibuka, the head of Sony.

• Ibuka wanted something businesspeople could use to relieve the boredom of long flights without disturbing other passengers.

• In June 1979, the *Walkman* was launched.

DIGITAL MUSIC

The *Diamond Rio* is typical of the first generation of MP3 players.

• Old recording machines made a copy of music on a tape or disc. If the recording was not perfect, crackles and hisses would be heard.

• Digital recording is different. The music is changed into numbers. It is the code that is recorded.

• A CD or MP3 player reads the code and uses it to create the music. Crackles and hisses that are not part of the code are ignored, so the music is perfect.

INVENTIONS FOR FUN

SCRABBLE®

When he lost his job as an architect during the Great Depression in 1931, Alfred Mosher Butts invented the game *Scrabble*. Butts calculated the letter frequency and points value for each letter by counting the frequency of letters on the front page of the New York Times.

MONOPOLY®

Monopoly was invented by American Charles B. Darrow. He sold his idea to Parker Brothers in 1935. *Monopoly* was a similar concept to Lizzie G. Magie's *Landlord's Game*, patented 1904. Magie's game was devised as a way to highlight the potential exploitation of tenants by greedy landlords.

ROLLERSKATE

In January, 1863, James Leonard Plimpton patented a four-wheeled roller skate that was capable of turning. Plimpton built a rollerskating floor in the office of his New York City furniture company.

LEGO®

In 1955, under the leadership of Godfred Kirk Christiansen, Lego launched the LEGO system of play that included LEGO automatic binding bricks. Christiansen's father, Ole Kirk, started the toy-making business in 1932. Today, approximately seven Lego sets are sold each second.

KALEIDOSCOPE

The kaleidoscope was patented by Scottish physicist Sir David Brewster in 1817. Kaleidoscopes use mirrors to reflect images of pieces of coloured glass in geometric designs. The design can be endlessly changed by rotating the end of the kaleidoscope.

BARBIE®

Barbara Millicent Roberts, or Barbie, as she is better known, was launched in 1959 by California toy company Mattel, Inc. Mattel calculates that every second, two Barbies are sold somewhere in the world.

INVENTION OF BASKETBALL

Basketball was invented in December, 1891, by James Naismith, a physical education instructor in Springfield, Massachusetts.
Basketball gets its name from the two bushel baskets (used for collecting peaches) that Naismith used as the goals.

INVENTING SPECIAL EFFECTS

- A new type of camera, called a *motion control camera*, was invented to make the first *Star Wars* movie in 1977.

- A motion control camera is a camera moved by a computer. The computer is programmed with the camera's movements, so the camera can go through exactly the same movements again and again.

- The camera films models of spacecraft and planets, one by one. Then, all the separate images are combined to form one scene.

AT THE MOVIES TIMELINE

1882 – Camera gun
Frenchman Étienne-Jules Marey is the first person to take a series of photographs quickly with one camera. The gun-like camera takes 12 photographs on a paper disc in one second. It was the forerunner of the movie camera.

1887 – Paper to film
American minister, Hannibal Goodwin, uses a strip of flexible film instead of light-sensitive paper to record images. Film quickly replaces paper.

1888 – First film
The first film is shot in Leeds, England, by Frenchman Louis Aimé Augustin Le Prince. It shows traffic crossing a bridge.

1891 – Kinetoscope
The American inventor Thomas Edison invents a machine called a *Kinetoscope* for showing films. Only one person can see the film at a time.

1895 – Cinema is born
The French brothers, Auguste and Louis Lumière, show films to the public for the first time. Cinemas quickly spread throughout France and all over the world.

1927 – Talkies
Warner Brothers make the first feature film with sound. It is called *The Jazz Singer*. Sound movies were called *talkies*.

1993 – Computer characters
Jurassic Park featured the most realistic computer-generated images (cgi) ever seen in a movie. Cgi was used to create life-like dinosaurs, which were blended with live action.

1995 – Computer movies
Pixar makes the first totally computer-generated movie, *Toy Story*.

2001 – Digital movies
The first movie shot entirely using digital cameras is *Star Wars: Attack of the Clones*.

Food and drink are essential needs for every human being. Without them, we would die. Just like everything else, however, that doesn't stop human beings from experimenting with and inventing new foods, new tastes, and new ways to grow, prepare, and store our food. Today, because we know that too much fat and sugar are bad for us, scientists are hard at work making our favorite foods and treats more healthy.

GROWING FOOD TIMELINE

1492 – New foods
Columbus discovers America. In the next two hundred years, potatoes, maize, tomatoes, tobacco, and cocoa reach the rest of the world.

1701 – Seed drill
Jethro Tull invents the seed drill in England. The drill sows seed in straight lines.

1701 – Fertilizer
The first *guano* (seabird manure) brought to Europe from South America is used as fertilizer.

1834 – Reaping machine
American Cyrus McCormick invents the horse-drawn reaping machine, which replaces workers using sickles and scythes to cut corn and make hay.

1837 – Steel plow
American John Deere invents the steel plow that can plow the soil of the American midwest without clogging. This makes it possible for people to settle and farm in this region.

1854 – Threshing machine
An improved American threshing machine can thresh 74 times more wheat in half an hour that a single worker.

1860 – Milking machine
With modern improvements of the milking machine, a farmer can milk six cows at a time and milk an entire herd without help.

1873 – Barbed wire
American Joseph Glidden perfects barbed wire, which makes fencing cheap.

1917 – Ford tractor
First mass-produced tractor made by Ford in 1917.

• See page 17 THE STORY OF GENETIC ENGINEERING: GM CROPS

INVENTING THE SANDWICH

- The sandwhich was invented in the 18th century by Englishman John Montagu, the 4th Earl of Sandwich.

- In 1762, Montagu played cards for 24 hours nonstop. It is believed that he ate beef between slices of toast so one of his hands was free to play cards at all times. Montagu's convenient snack was named the *sandwich* after the inventive earl.

INVENTING COCA-COLA

- Described as the world's "best known taste," the drink we now know as *Coca-Cola®* was invented by pharmacist Dr John Stith Pemberton, in Atlanta, Georgia.

- On May 8, 1886, a jug of Permberton's syrup was sampled at Jacobs' Pharmacy and pronounced, "Excellent" by the lucky "guinea pigs" who were gathered there. Carbonated water was added to the syrup to produce a drink that was both "delicious and refreshing." The new product was immediately put on sale for five cents a glass.

- The inventor's partner, Frank M. Robertson, suggested the name *Coca-Cola* and correctly thought that, "the two Cs would look well in advertising."

The famous Coca-Cola trademark was penned in Robertson's unique script.

LOUIS PASTEUR 1822–1895

Nationality: French
Profession: Scientist

Biographical information: The young Louis Pasteur did not impress as a student, but classes given by a brilliant chemistry teacher were to change his life. After studying at the famous *École Normale Supérieure* in Paris, he became the Dean of the Faculty of Science at the University of Lille.

Eureka moment: While studying the fermentation process of wine and vinegar, he made his greatest discovery. Fermentation and decay are caused by microscopic living organisms. By heating wine to about 140° F, he killed off the unwanted yeast cells that caused the product to spoil.

Most famous discovery: Pasteur showed that invisible organisms can spoil food and cause disease. Pasteurization, the process he invented of making liquids hot enough to kill any harmful organisms without destroying their food value, is still used today, particularly in milk production. It is used to kill bacteria that can cause tuberculosis in humans.

Other discoveries: Vaccinations,

including a vaccine for the killer disease rabies, developed from the brain tissue of infected animals. Pasteur cured a boy who had been bitten by a rabid dog and was hailed as a hero.

• See page 23 EDWARD JENNER

CLARENCE BIRDSEYE 1886–1956

Nationality: American

Profession: Naturalist

Biographical information:
Clarence Birdseye was born in Brooklyn, New York in 1886. He studied biology at college, but left to work as a field naturalist for the US government in northern Canada.

Eureka moment: In Labrador, in 1912, Birdseye watched native Americans fishing through holes chipped in an icy lake. As fish were pulled out, they were immediately frozen by the intense cold air. Birdseye realised that speedy chilling solved the main problem with frozen food—ice.

Most famous invention: When food is frozen slowly, long, sharp crystals of ice are formed which cut into the food causing it to break up when defrosted. It took Birdseye eight years to work out how to chill food quickly enough to stop the daggers of ice forming. By 1930, Birdseye's machine which squeezed pre-packed food between two very cold plates was ready to go into

Clarence Birdseye (in the white lab coat) experiments with a huge dehydration machine.

production. However, home freezers were still very rare.

It would be 1955, before Birdseye's invention was finally a worldwide success.

THE INVENTION OF THE CHIP

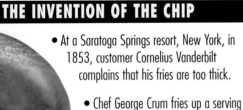

- At a Saratoga Springs resort, New York, in 1853, customer Cornelius Vanderbilt complains that his fries are too thick.

- Chef George Crum fries up a serving of paper-thin, crunchy, crisp potatoes. Called *Saratoga Chips*, they quickly became a favorite. Crum invents the potato chip!

- Chips as we now know them became popular in the 1920s when Mrs. Scudder mass produced them and sold them in waxed paper bags.

- In 1926, Lay's potato chips were the first successfully marketed national brand.

INVENTING THE CORNFLAKE

- American Will Kellogg worked at his family's health resort that promoted healthy vegetarian food.

- In 1894, while experimenting with boiled wheat, he discovered that when crushed between rollers, wheat that had been previously soaked for a long time broke into flakes.

- *Toasted Corn Flakes* were sold first by mail order and then through shops. In 1906, Will parted company with his brother John who objected to the addition of sugar and salt to the cereal.

- 20 years later, Will Kellogg was a cornflake tycoon and one of the richest men in America.

CHOCOLATE CHIPS BY ACCIDENT

- One day in 1930, while preparing a batch of *Butter Drop Do* cookies, American Ruth Wakefield substituted a semi-sweet Nestle chocolate bar, cut up into bits, for the usual cooking chocolate she used in her cookie recipe.

- Unlike the cooking chocolate, the pieces of chocolate did not melt when they were baked, they only softened. The chocolate chip cookie was born.

CHOCOLATE DISCOVERY & INVENTION TIMELINE

c 1000 BC
Chocolate is produced from cocoa beans. It is believed that the Olmec Indians of Central America were the first to grow cocoa beans as a crop.

Early 1500s
Christopher Columbus and later the Spanish explorer Hernando Cortez record seeing cocoa being used and bought and sold during their explorations in the Americas.

1544
Mayan nobles bring gifts of ready-to-drink, beaten chocolate to Prince Philip of Spain. It will be 100 years before Spain and Portugal export the drink to the rest of Europe.

The Spanish add cane sugar and vanilla to their cocoa drink, and coca becomes popular as a medicine.

Late 1600s
Eating solid chocolate is introduced in Europe in the form of rolls and cakes, served in chocolate stores.

1753
Swedish naturalist Carolus Linnaeus, dissatisfied with the word *cocoa*, renames it *theobroma*, Greek for *food of the gods*.

1765
Irish chocolate-maker John Hanan imports cocoa beans to the USA. Hanan and fellow American Dr. James Baker build America's first chocolate mill making Baker's chocolate.

1828
Conrad Van Houten invents the cocoa press.

1847
Joseph Fry and Son create a paste that can be molded to produce the first modern chocolate bar.

1876
Milk chocolate is invented by Daniel Peter of Vevey, Switzerland after eight years of experimenting.

• The timeline continues on page 41.

THE COMPUTER

Computers are now used in nearly every part of our lives, and yet the computer has only been around for about 80 years. One hundred years ago, mechanical machines that did calculations were used, but it was only at the end of the 1930s that electronic computers appeared. The first computers were large machines designed for use in laboratories, in industry, and for defense. Once computer could fill up a whole room. In 1974, it became possible to have a computer in your home.

The Apple Macintosh, or Mac, was the first computer to have what is known as a desktop-type screen with icons.

ANCIENT COMPUTER

- The abacus was invented in the period 3000–1000 BC by the Babylonians (ancient race of people living in the area that is modern-day Iraq).

- This early counting machine made up of beads on rods can be said to be the first step in the development of the computer.

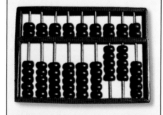

THE POTENTIAL OF AN INVENTION

At first, not everyone could see the computer's potential.

"I think there is a world market for maybe five computers."
– Thomas Watson, Chairman of IBM, 1943.

"There is no reason anyone in the right state of mind will want a computer in their home."
– Ken Olson, President of Digital Equipment Corp., 1977.

THE FIRST COMPUTERS

1946 – ENIAC
Electronic Numerical Integrator and Computer is the first electronic and programable computer. It contained over 17,000 vacuum tubes. Eniac occupied a room 50 feet by 30 feet.

ENIAC

1951 – UNIVAC 1
The world's first electronic computer goes on sale. It was created by John Eckert and John Mauchly. It was used by the US government to help gather material for the national census.

UNIVAC

1977 – Apple II
The first successful personal computer goes on sale. It was made by Apple® Computers, Inc. It was the first computer to have a color screen and its own keyboard.

1983 – Apple Lisa
The first computer, also created by Apple, to use a mouse and pull-down menus.

APPLE II

A factory worker makes vacuum tubes.

VACUUM TUBES

The main electronic parts of early computers were called *vacuum tubes*, or simply *valves*, because they controlled the flow of electricity.

Transistors are made of materials called *semiconductors*.

1947 - TRANSISTORS

The first prototype transistor was invented at the Bell laboratories in the USA. The transistor acts as an electronic switch, and once it is perfected in the 1950s, quickly replaces the vacuum tube.

This microchip, held in the jaws of an ant, contains thousands of components.

1960s - MICROCHIPS

In the late 1960s, the integrated circuit was developed. Thousands of transistors and other electric components could be built onto a tiny silicon chip, or *microchip*.

1968 - MICROPROCESSORS

In 1968, Ted Hoff of Intel was asked to come up with a design for a new calculator chip that could do several jobs at once. He came up with the idea of the microprocessor. Launched in 1971, the microprocessor made it possible to build much smaller computers.

INVENTIONS FOR THE COMPUTER

1964 — Inkjet printer

The first inkjet printer is invented. Inkjet printers spray fast-drying ink on paper.

1965 — Mouse

US engineer Doug Engelbart and his team at the Human Factors Research Center of the Stanford Research Institute, design and develop the computer mouse.

1976 — Laser printer

First laser printer introduced.

1991 — Digital camera

Kodak produces the first digital camera, the *DCS100*. The photos have to be stored in a separate piece of equipment.

Today's digital cameras collect more than 5 million separate pieces of information every time you take a picture.

Computer mouse

COMPUTERS ALL AROUND

Today, a computer is in almost every electrical item we use.

MOBILE PHONE

The computer in a mobile phone determines the closest transmitter to your current position.

CAR

An in-car computer controls the most economical use of gas in most modern cars.

VIDEO CAMERA

All modern video cameras include an auto focus function that examines what it can see, detects the edges of each item coming through the lens, and adjusts the focus to keep pictures sharp.

AIRPLANE

There are probably more computers in an airplane than any other vehicle. Computers control everything from the speed and height of the plane, to the running of the in-flight movie and the cooking of any meals served.

ALAN TURING 1912–1954

Nationality: British

Profession: Mathematician and computer expert

Biographical information: Turing was born in 1912. He had a gift for mathematics, which he studied at Cambridge University.

Eureka moment: In 1924, university student Alan Turing wrote an essay in which he described a machine that is the basis of all computers in the world today. It was the first idea for a computer to include memory, a processor, and a way of storing information on tape.

Most famous invention:

Turing's work as a mathematian was stopped by World War II. He was taken to Bletchley Park, in England, where he led a team trying to find a way to crack the Enigma code used by Germany, Italy and Japan. In 1943, Turing designed a computer called the *Colossus* that helped to decipher the German codes, which helped to win the war.

Other inventions: After World War II, Turing continued working on computers. In 1950, he wrote an article in which he said that a computer could have the same intelligence as any person. .

COMPUTERS TIMELINE

1959 – First minicomputer

Digital Equipment Corporation produce an early minicomputer the *PDP-1*. Selling for $120,000, it was a fraction of the cost of mainframe computers. The later model *PDP-8* in 1965 uses the recently invented integrated circuit and sells for $20,000.

1967 – Computer keyboard

Keyboards are used for data entry.

1968 – INTEL

Intel is formed. The company will grow to become one of the world's largest and most important computer processor manufacturers.

1970 – Floppy disk

The floppy disk produced by IBM.

1971 – Microprocessor

The first microprocessor is produced.

1974 – Personal computer

The first personal computer, the *Altair 8800*, goes on sale. It is sold as a kit, so the customer has to put the computer together before they use it.

1975 – Microsoft®

Bill Gates and Paul G. Allen form Microsoft and adapt BASIC language for use on the Altair PC.

1976 – Apple®

Apple Computers is founded by Steve Wozniak and Steve Jobs.

1981 – IBM® pc

IBM launches their *Personal Computer* (IBM PC), which uses *Microsoft Disc Operating System* (MS-DOS).

1982 – CD

Philips Electronics and Sony Corporation work together to invent the CD.

1984 – Macintosh®

Apple launches the *Macintosh Computer*, designed to appeal to those who are not computer experts.

1985 – Windows®

Microsoft releases the first version of the operating system, called *Windows*.

1995 – Windows 95

Microsoft releases *Windows 95*, which fully integrates MS-DOS with Windows.

INTERNET TIMELINE

1960s–1980s – Arpanet
A team at the US Advanced Research Projects Agency (ARPA) develop a communications network between researchers and scientists in the US.

Other organizations will join the network throughout the 1970s and early 1980s, and the network will grow and grow.

1971 – The first email
The first email is sent by computer engineer Ray Tomlinson.

1973–1974 – Inventing the Internet
Vint Cerf and Bob Kahn design the Internet – a network of computers and cables. They also define the IP (Internet Protocol), the way information is be sent on the Internet.

1979 – Emotions
Adding emotions to email messages is suggested, such as –) to show something is 'tongue in cheek'.
By the early 1980s :-) and :-(are in widespread use.

1980 – First virus
The first virus is accidentally released onto ARPAnet, bringing the whole network to a halt.

1983 – The Internet
The Internet is launched and made available to everyone.

The Domain Name System (DNS) takes you where you need to be on the Internet using a web address. DNS is invented by Paul Mockapetris.

Computer expert Fred Cohen invents the term *computer virus*.

1987 – MP3 files
The development of the MP3 file format begins at the Fraunhofer Institut in Germany. It allows music and speech recordings to be compressed and will be used by many people on the Internet to easily copy and trade their music collections.

• The INTERNET TIMELINE continues on page 43.

T he Internet is a worldwide collection of computers connected by cables, telephone lines, and satellites. It allows people to send electronic messages, called *emails*, to anyone else who is connected, interact with other computer users wherever they are in the world, and to look at information created by both large organizations and private individuals, via the World Wide Web.

TIM BERNERS-LEE

Nationality: English

Profession: Computer scientist

Biographical information:
Berners-Lee was born in London, England in 1955. Interested in computers, he went to Oxford University. While at Oxford, he built his own computer from old electronic parts of a TV. Both of his parents worked in the computer industry.

Eureka moment: Berners-Lee developed a program called *Enquire* to help him access varied pieces of information needed in his work. The information was stored in files that contained connections, called *hypertext links*.

Most famous invention: The World Wide Web. In 1989, while working at CERN (European Centre for Nuclear Research) in Geneva, Switzerland, Berners-Lee wrote a program that allowed CERN's scientists to share their work

TIM BERNERS-LEE

through a global hypertext document system. The Web was released to the world via the Internet in 1991.

Other inventions: In 1994, Berners-Lee founded the World Wide Web Consortium. The consortium's goal is to lead the Web to its full potential in the future.

INVENTION OF EMAIL

In 1971, US computer scientist Ray Tomlinson created a computer program for sending messages on the ARPAnet network. The program would become email, one of the main ways of communicating on the Internet.

• The first test message was sent between two machines that were physically next to each other, but only connected by ARPAnet.

• Today, Tomlinson cannot remember what the first email said, but he jokes it was probably just something like, "QWERTYUIOP" (the top line of letters on a keyboard).

• Probably the first email message sent to another person on ARPAnet was one announcing the new service and telling people to use @, the symbol Tomlinson chose to separate user names from host computer names.

INVENTING THE INTERNET

• Internet pioneers Vint Cerf and Bob Kahn invented the Internet Protocol, the way of sending little "packets" of information through the Internet network.

• A packet is like a postcard containing information.

• If the packet has the right address, it can be given to any computer connected to the Internet, and the computer can figure out which cable to send the packet down so it gets to where it needs to go.

MOSAIC

- In 1993, the world's first user-friendly web browser, called *Mosaic*, was developed by American Mark Andreessen and a team at the US National Center for Supercomputing Applications (NCSA).

- Mosaic used a point-and-click application that made it easy for people to navigate the World Wide Web.

- By 1994, Mosaic had several million users.

PONG

- In 1972, the Atari Corporation was founded by US computer engineers Nolan Bushnell, Ted Dabney, and Al Alcorn.

- In 1972, Bushnell and team invented the video game *Pong*, based on ping-pong (table tennis).

- Two on-screen paddles hit a ball back and forth across the screen.

- *Pong* became hugely popular as an arcade-style, coin-operated game, and went on to be produced in a home version.

THE NEWEST 2 PLAYER VIDEO SKILL GAME

PONG

from ATARI CORPORATION
SYZYGY ENGINEERED
The Team That Pioneered Video Technology

1970s poster advertising the revolutionary new game, *Pong*.

INTERNET TIMELINE

1988 – Internet worm
Robert Morris, a US science student unleashes an Internet worm (a program that propagates itself across a network) onto the Internet. The Morris Worm brings 6,000 computers to a halt.

1989 – Inventing www
Tim Berners-Lee invents the World Wide Web—a way for computer users to access many different types of information from different sources.

1991 – WWW on the net
The World Wide Web is launched and made available to the world via the Internet.

1992 – Surfing
The term *surfing the Internet* is used for the first time, by American librarian and Internet expert Jean Armour Polly.

1993 – Mosaic
The first web browser is created. It is called *Mosaic*.

1994 – Yahoo!®
The Yahoo! search engine is created in April 1994 by David Filo and Jerry Yang, two PhD students at Stanford University, in California. They invent the directory as a way of keeping track of their interests and finding websites for their friends.

1995 – Internet Explorer®
Launched in July 1995 as part of the Windows 95 package, Internet Explorer 1.0 helps make the Internet accessible to more people.

1995 – Online music
RealAudio® is launched. This software makes it possible for Internet users to listen to live music and radio stations online.

1995 – Online bookstore
Amazon.com® is launched by US computer scientist Jeff Bezos. The company is started in Bezos' garage.

2000 – Web movie
The science-fiction movie *Quantum Project* is the first movie made specifically to be seen on the Internet instead of in a movie theater.

2002 – Internet users
The number of Internet users is estimated at 604,111,719 worldwide.

TIMELINE: INVENTION OF COMPUTER GAMES

1889 – NINTENDO®
The Nintendo company is founded in Japan. It makes playing cards.

1958 – FIRST "COMPUTER GAME"
William A. Higinbotham of the Brookhaven National Laboratory in New York uses an analog computer, control boxes and an oscilloscope to create *Tennis for Two*, a game to amuse visitors to the laboratory.

1962 – SPACEWAR!
A team at the Massachusetts Institute of Technology (MIT), invent a game as part of a program to demonstrate the new *PDP-1* computer. The game, which would now look extremely simple, involves players moving spaceships and firing torpedoes.

1972 – PONG
Atari creates *Pong*.

1977 – MISSILE ATTACK
Mattel releases the first handheld game, but it uses small lights rather than a screen to display graphics.

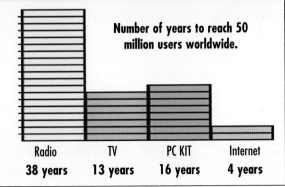

1980 – BATTLEZONE
The first 3D game is produced. *Battlezone* is such a breakthrough that the US government uses it to train troops.

1989 – NINTENDO GAMEBOY
Video games go handheld with the release of the first Nintendo Gameboy.

1994 – PLAYSTATION®
Sony releases the PlayStation, but only in Japan. It reaches the rest of the world the following year.

2000 – PLAYSTATION 2
It is even more successful than the original PlayStation, selling out worldwide within days.

Nintendo sells its one hundred millionth Gameboy.

2002 - X-BOX®
Microsoft enters the console market as it launches the X-Box.

- See page 54
OSCILLOSCOPE

A FAST-GROWING INVENTION

In 1998, the US Department of Commerce report *The Emerging Digital Economy* stated that, "The Internet's pace of adoption eclipses all other technologies that preceded it."

When radio was invented, it took 38 years to reach 50 million users. The Internet took just 4 years.

Number of years to reach 50 million users worldwide.

Radio	TV	PC KIT	Internet
38 years	13 years	16 years	4 years

• The TIMELINE continues on page 45.

ROBOTS

The word *robot* was first used by the Czech writer Karel Capek. It means *forced labor* and is a good way of describing what robots are for. Robots can do many jobs that human beings can do, but they can also tackle jobs that a human would find too difficult or dangerous. Robots are currently used in factories, they explore outer space and the inside of volcanoes, and they appear in our homes as toys or cyber (robotic) pets.

RoboSapien

The *AIBO®* robotic pet dog. AIBO dogs can even play soccer.

CYBER PETS

A robot dog first made an appearance at the New York World's Fair in 1939. Today, cyber pets can behave like real animals.

AIBO DOGS
The latest cyber dogs made by Sony can play, walk, obey spoken commands, and even recognise the voices and faces of their owners.

ROBOSAPIEN
This human-like cyber pet can run, dance, throw things, pick things up, and try karate.

TAKARA AQUAROID FISH
This cyber pet can be put into an aquarium. It looks like a fish, moves away from strong light, and swims at two different speeds.

TOMY *HUMAN DOG*
This cyber pet is built by Tomy. It can walk, sit, sing songs, and has 16 different personalities.

ROBOT SECURITY GUARD

- *MOSRO* patrols factories and shopping centers.

- *MOSRO* can detect gas, smoke, and movement with a camera and infrared detectors.

- *MOSRO* issues warnings in over 20 languages.

This is the MOSRO MINI mobile security robot. It is just 11 inches tall.

DOMESTIC ROBOTS

2002 – MARON
It can detect intruders in a house, take photographs and can operate dishwashers and video recorders. It can be controlled with a mobile phone.

2003 – ROBOMOW RL1000
It can mow lawns without any help, and cut grass to six different heights. It is just over 12 inches high.

2003 – CYE ROBOT
It can carry dishes, deliver letters, and help guests find their way around a house. It can be controlled using the internet.

MARON

INVENTING HAZBOTS

Robots that do jobs that are too dangerous for people are sometimes called *hazbots*.

RADIOACTIVITY

In 1999, a hazbot called *Pioneer* was used at the Chernobyl nuclear power station, the site of the worst nuclear accident in history. *Pioneer* went into the burned-out, radioactive power station to test for levels of radioactivity and to test the structure of the remaining building. *Pioneer* was built by a team from the Carnegie Mellon University and Redzone Robotics.

BOMB DISPOSAL

The British army have used bomb disposal robots since the early 70s. The first was called *Wheelbarrow*.

NATURAL HAZARDS

Robots are used to investigate volcanoes. *Dante II* explored an Alaskan volcano in 1994. It can be remotely controlled or it can move by itself. It was developed by the Carnegie Mellon University.

FIREFIGHTING

Robots are used to fight fires, because they are not affected by the heat and smoke. *Robug-3* is a fire-fighting robot designed at Portsmouth University in the UK. It has eight legs, and suckers on its feet allow it to climb walls and across ceilings. It can also pull very heavy objects.

THE INVENTION OF MINI-ROBOTS

At the US Department of Energy's Sandia National Laboratories, scientists are developing the world's smallest autonomous, untethered robot.

- The mini-robot has 8 kilobytes of memory, is less than an inch high and weighs about an ounce.

- The mini-robot is powered by watch batteries and enhancements could include a miniature camera, a microphone, or chemical sniffers.

- The mini-robot travels on two track wheels at a speed of 20 inches per minute.

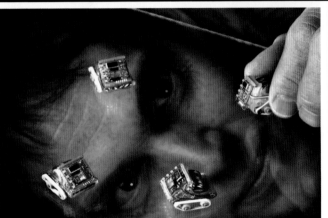

The mini-robots could travel in swarms like insects and fit into tiny spaces.

- Future uses could include detecting chemical or biological weapons; disabling land mines; or even spying, taking photographs of secret papers without being detected.

ROBOTS IN SPACE

1997 — CASSINI-HUYGENS
Studying the planet Saturn, its rings and moons.

2003 — SMART 1
Searching the moon for frozen water, new minerals, and chemicals.

2004 — ROSETTA
Sent to investigate a comet's surface in 2014.

2003 — BEAGLE 2
Designed to investigate the surface of Mars, but disappeared after landing.

2003 — SPIRIT AND OPPORTUNITY
Studied the soil and rocks of Mars.

GEORGE DEVOL

Nationality: American

Profession: Engineer and inventor

Biographical information: Devol was born in February 1912, in Louisville, Kentucky. In 1939, Devol designed and built an automatic counter at the New York World's Fair. The counter kept a record of the number of visitors.

Most famous invention: The first industrial robot. In 1954, Devol invented the first programmable robot. He did not use the word *robot*, but *universal automation*. Devol founded the world's first robot building company that built robots called *unimation*, for lifting and stacking hot pieces of metal in a car factory.

Other inventions: During World War II, Devol helped to build systems that could protect aircraft from radar. They were used during the D-Day landings in Europe in 1944.

ROBOTICS TIMELINE

1977 — Voyagers
The deep space explorers *Voyagers 1* and 2 are launched from the Kennedy Space Flight Center.

1979 — Stanford Cart
The *Stanford Cart* is improved with a better system for 'seeing' things.

1981 — Direct drive arm
The first "direct drive arms" are built. They have motors in the joints of the arms. This makes them faster and more accurate than older robotic arms. They are designed by Takeo Kanade, Professor of Robotics at Carnegie Mellon University.

1989 — Genghis
A walking robot, called *Genghis*, is shown for the first time at the Massachusetts Institute of Technology (MIT).

1992 — Robot wars
Combats between robots, sometimes called *BattleBots*, begin. The first "Robot Wars" take place in 1994.

1994 — Dante II
A robot called *Dante II* walks down a volcano in Alaska.

1996 — Robotuna
The first robot fish is built. It is designed by Professor Michael Triantafyllou of the Massachusetts Institute of Technology (MIT). It is hoped that underwater robots will be able to explore parts of the ocean where humans cannot reach.

1997 — Sojourner
The robotic rover *Sojourner* begins its exploration of the surface of Mars.

1998 — The Furby
The *Furby* goes on sale. It is the first robot toy that can respond to commands.

2000 — Asimo
The human-like robot, called *Asimo*, is built by Honda. It is four feet tall, walks on legs and can even walk around corners. It is designed to help around the house.

INVENTORS

An inventor is anyone who thinks of something new to make or a new way to make or do something. We do not know the names of most of the inventors who have influenced our lives, or exactly when they made their breakthroughs. But many inventors are famous, and we even know about the 'eureka moment' when they had their brilliant idea.

ARCHIMEDES OF SYRACUSE 287–212 BC

The 'Archimedes Portrait' by Domenico Fetti, painted in 1620.

Nationality: Greek

Profession: Mathematician

Biographical information: Archimedes was born and worked in the city of Syracuse in Sicily, although he studied at Alexandria, Egypt. He was killed when Roman soldiers conquered Syracuse.

Most famous invention: While wondering about how to test if a crown was made of pure gold, Archimedes discovered the *principle of buoyancy* — if an object is placed in a fluid, it will displace its own volume of fluid. This is now known as *Archimedes' principle*.

Eureka moment: Archimedes had the original "eureka" moment. Getting into a bath he noticed that the water rose up the sides. His body was displacing its own volume of water. He raced into the street, without any clothes, shouting, "Eureka" (I've found it)!

• See page 52 ARCHIMEDEAN SCREW

GALILEO GALILEI 1564–1642

Nationality: Italian

Profession: Mathematician

Biographical information: The son of a musician, Galileo went to the University of Pisa to study medicine, but eventually became a professor of mathematics. During the 1630s, Galileo was arrested and imprisoned by the Catholic Church because of his scientific views.

Most famous invention: Galileo is widely considered to be the founder of modern experimental science. He established the principle that scientific theories should be based on data obtained from experiments.

Eureka moment: Galileo was able to devise a mathematical formula to describe the motion of falling objects. The story that he dropped identical weights of iron and feathers from the Leaning Tower of Pisa may not be true, but Galileo did establish that all objects fall at the same speed, no matter what their weight.

Other discoveries: Galileo was also interested in astronomy. He did not invent the telescope, but he built his own in 1609. Galileo was able to observe the craters on Earth's moon, he discovered that Jupiter has four moons, and he was the first person to describe the rings of Saturn.

• See page 18 for more information on Galileo's life and work.

Galileo, on an Italian 2000 lire banknote.

LEONARDO DA VINCI 1452–1519

Leonardo Da Vinci

Nationality: Italian

Profession: Artist

Biographical information: Da Vinci was apprenticed to a sculptor and worked as a painter for the rulers of Florence, Milan, and France. He produced some famous paintings, including the *Mona Lisa*.

Da Vinci filled thousands of pages of notebooks with drawings and notes about everything he saw around him. He studied human anatomy, military engineering, the flight of birds, and the movement of water.

Most famous invention: Leonardo's notebooks contained drawings and ideas which would not be put into practice for hundreds of years, such as parachutes, canals, armored cars, and submarines.

Eureka moment: Da Vinci showed that by drawing what he imagines, an inventor can inspire future generations to make these visions real.

SIR ISAAC NEWTON 1642–1727

Nationality: English
Profession: Mathematician

Biographical information:
Newton went to Cambridge University in 1661, but his studies were interrupted by an outbreak of plague that closed the university for two years. During this period of forced idleness, Newton did most of his best thinking. In 1667, he was appointed professor of mathematics at Cambridge.

- Most of his work is contained in his books *Principia Mathematica* (1687) and *Opticks* (1704).

Most famous discovery:
Newton is best known for his *theory of universal gravitation*—that there is an attractive force between all the objects in the universe, and this force is called *gravity*. Newton used his theory to discover the mathematical laws that govern the motion of every object in the universe. The movement of any object, be it a pick-up truck or a planet, can be explained and predicted by what is known as *Newtonian physics*.

Other discoveries:
- A comprehensive theory of light that explained how lenses worked and how white light could be split into colors.

- A system of arithmetic called *calculus*.

- Newton built a reflecting telescope that used a curved mirror to give a better image.

Newton Stories:
- Newton is supposed to have thought up the *theory of gravitation* after watching an apple fall from a tree.

- While studying light, Newton pushed blunt needles into the corners of his eyes to see what effect squashing his eyeballs had on his vision.

Sir Isaac Newton

• See page 18
INVENTION OF THE TELESCOPE

A TO Z INVENTORS

Franklin, Benjamin
American statesman, scientist and writer Benjamin Franklin was fascinated by the discovery of electricity. In 1752, convinced that thunderstorms were electric, he proved it by flying a special kite into a storm. The lightning struck the kite and electricity travelled down the string. Franklin realized that buildings could be protected from thunderbolts if the electricity was conducted through a metal spike on the roof of a building to the ground via a thick wire. Franklin had invented a lightning conductor.

Galilei, Galileo
Galileo was so intrigued by the swinging of the incense burner in Pisa's cathedral, it inspired him to work with pendulums. Galileo measured the time it took to make a complete swing and discovered that it took the same amount of time to get back to where it started, even when the size of the swing changed. Galileo experimented with pendulums for many years, but by the time he thought of using a pendulum's even swing to keep a clock running smoothly, he was old and totally blind.

Gillette, King C
Advised by a colleague to invent "something that would be used and thrown away," Gillette invented the disposable razor blade and new safety razor. Constantly having to buy new blades was not popular with customers, but never having to use a "cut-throat" razor again was! Gillette founded his razor blade company in 1903.

Halley, Edmond
In 1717, English astronomer Edmond Halley invented the first diving bell in which people could stay underwater for long periods. Earlier devices, primarily built for attemps to retrieve sunken treasure, had not been successful. Air was supplied to Halley's diving bell in barrels with weights to make them sink.

• See page 18
HALLEY'S COMET

INVENTORS

Kwolek, Stephanie

Pound for pound, Stephanie Kwolek's invention of Kevlar is 5 times stronger than steel. It is also chemical and flame resistant. Kevlar, best known for its use in bullet-proof vests and crash helmets was developed in the 1960s when chemist Kwolek was working in the laboratory of US company DuPont Textiles.

Leclanché, Georges

In 1866, French engineer Leclanché invented the sealed, dry cell battery that is still used in many flashlights today. Until the invention of the Leclanché cell, people were restricted to Volta's battery that contained a liquid that had to be constantly filled up.

Mars, Frank

In 1911, Frank Mars and his wife Ethel began making and selling butter-cream sweets from their home in Tacoma, Washington. In 1920, Frank invented the Mars bar when he came up with the idea of producing malted chocolate milkshakes in a solid form that could be enjoyed anywhere.

Mercator, Gerhard

Around 1568, Flemish cartographer Gerhard Mercator produced a map that gave sailors constant compass directions as straight lines. The Mercator projection provided a flat, peeled view of the globe. The map is very accurate for navigators, but showing the curved earth on flat paper causes distortions and makes countries near the poles look too big.

JOHANNES GUTENBERG 1400-1468

Nationality: German

Profession: Jeweler/craftsman

Biographical information: Gutenberg was born in Mainz and trained as a goldsmith. He lived and worked in Strasbourg between 1430 and 1444, then returned to Mainz.

Most famous invention: The process of printing with moveable type and a printing press based on existing screw presses used to crush juice from grapes and olives.

Inventor at work: After 20 years of secret work to perfect all the necessary processes, Gutenberg printed and published his first book, a Latin Bible, in 1455. Money disputes with his financial backer, Johann Fust, caused him to lose his business.

• See page 8
THE INVENTION OF PRINTING

JOSEPH AND JACQUES MONTGOLFIER

Joseph: 1740–1810

Jacques: 1745–1799

Nationality: French

Profession: Paper-makers

Biographical information: The Montgolfier brothers worked in their father's paper factory in Annonay, France.

Eureka moment: Joseph and Jacques noticed how flames sent scraps of paper floating up the chimney. They became convinced that a large bag filled with hot air would rise.

Most famous invention: The first hot air balloon. On September 19, 1783, a sheep, a duck, and a cockerel became the first living creatures to fly in free flight or in a wicker basket suspended from a Montgolfier balloon. On November 21, 1783, Jean Francois Pilatre de Rosier and the Marquis d'Arlandes flew over Paris for 23 minutes in a Montgolfier balloon—the first human flight.

The Montgolfier balloon was made of fabric lined with paper. It was 33 feet across.

• See page 29
THE BALLOON
INVENTORS

SAMUEL MORSE 1791-1872

Nationality: American

Profession: Artist and inventor

Biographical information: Morse was born in Massachusetts. His father worked in the church and wrote geography books. Morse went to Yale when he was 14 years old. He earned money painting pictures of his friends and teachers. He studied art in England and became a well-known painter.

Most famous invention: Morse's interest in electricity led to his invention of the electrical telegraph and morse code.

Eureka moment: Morse demonstrated his telegraph to the American Congress, and in 1843, they give him $30,000 to build a telegraph line from Washington, D.C. to Baltimore

Other inventions: The bathometer, used to find out how deep rivers and lakes were.

• See page 30 MORSE CODE

LOUIS BRAILLE 1809-1852

Nationality: French

Profession: Teacher

Biographical information: Louis Braille was blinded at the age of three in an accident at his father's harness shop. In 1819, he went to the National Institute for Blind Children in Paris and later became a teacher there.

Eureka moment: At school in Paris, Braille learned of a system called *night writing*, invented by Captain Charles Barbier, for battlefield communications during the night. In 1824, just 15 years old, Braille developed his own system, using Barbier's as a starting point.

Most famous invention: A system of reading and writing for the blind

using raised dots in a six-dot matrix system. Braille's system was first published in 1829.

Braille is read using the fingertips.

THOMAS ALVA EDISON 1847-1931

Nationality: American

Profession: Inventor

Biographical information: After being expelled from school for pranks, Edison was educated at home by his mother. He began experimenting with batteries and electricity when he was ten. He built his own telegraph, and his first job was as a telegraph operator.

Most famous invention: Edison was already well known in the USA, but his 1877 invention of the phonograph made him world famous. The phonograph was

the first device that could play pre-recorded music.

Inventor at work: In 1876, Edison decided to become a full-time inventor. He built the world's first industrial research laboratory, which he called an *inventions factory*, in Menlo Park, New Jersey.

Other inventions: Edison also invented the electric light bulb. Edison sometimes made as many as 400 inventions a year including the incandescent electric lamp, the microphone, and the kinetoscope.

Edison patented 1093 inventions.

• See pages 31 and 36 for more information on Edison's inventing work.

GEORGE EASTMAN 1854-1932

Nationality: American

Profession: Photographic film manufacturer

Biographical information: After leaving school, Eastman worked in

insurance and banking while pursuing his hobby of photography. In 1880, he perfected a method of making photographic plates and set up a factory where he soon developed transparent film.

Most famous invention: In 1900, Eastman launched the *Box Brownie* camera. It was so cheap, only a dollar, including film, that everybody could afford to buy one, making photography available to all.

The first Kodak camera (Eastman invented and trademarked the name *Kodak*) marked the beginning of amateur photography.

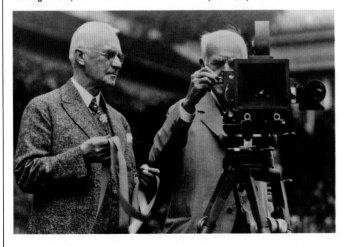

George Eastman (left) and Thomas Edison introduce color motion pictures to the world in 1928.

• See page 9 for THE INVENTION OF PHOTOGRAPHY

Perignon, Dom
Benedictine monk Dom Perignon is credited with inventing champagne in around 1670, but other winemakers of the Champagne region of France probably contributed to its development. The special method of fermentation, known as *méthode champenoise*, produces the carbon dioxide that creates the bubbles.

Richter, Charles F.
American seismologist Charles F. Richter developed his numbering system for measuring earthquakes in 1935. An earthquake measuring below 2 on the Richter scale would be recorded by equipment but not felt by a person. An earthquake measuring 8 or more would be devastating.

Roosevelt, Theodore

While on a hunting expedition in 1902, president Theodore "Teddy" Roosevelt refused to shoot a defenseless bear cub. The story enhanced the popularity of the already popular president. Morris Michtom, a New York retailer cashed in on the incident by selling plush-covered bears with button eyes and jointed limbs. He called them *Teddy's Bears*. A huge success, they soon became known as *Teddy Bears*.

Rubik, Erno

Hungarian design professor, Erno Rubik, invented the Rubik's Cube. Popular during the early 1980s, over 150 million cubes were sold (100 million real units and 50 million fakes). Once twisted from its original arrangement, the puzzle had 43 quintillion possible configurations.

Schueller, Eugene

In 1936, French chemist Eugene Schueller produced the first suntan lotion at his company L'Oréal. Designer Coco Chanel made suntanning fashionable around this time. Today, the oil is sold around the world as *Ambre Solaire*.

Semple, William Finlay

On December 28, 1869, William Semple of Mt Vernon, Ohio, became the first person to patent a chewing gum—US patent 98,304.

Sinclair, Clive

In 1985, British inventor Clive Sinclair invented the *C5*, a battery-powered bike. The *C5* had a top speed of 15 mph, a range of 20 miles, and took eight hours to recharge the batteries. Unfortunately for Sinclair, consumers were not impressed with his new type of vehicle, and the invention flopped.

INVENTORS

MARIE CURIE 1867–1934

Nationality: Polish

Profession: Physicist

Biographical information: Marie Sklodowska studied physics and math at university in Paris. In 1895, she married the French scientist Pierre Curie.

Most famous invention:
In 1898, the Curies discovered the radioactive elements radium, thorium, and polonium, named for Marie's homeland. In 1903, they shared the Nobel Prize for physics with Henri Becquerel. In 1911,

Marie Curie was awarded the Nobel Prize for chemistry for her continuing work on radium and radioactivity. Doctors found that radium could be used to treat cancer through radiotherapy.

Eureka moment: The discovery of radium involved breaking down and refining several tonnes of a mineral called *pitchblende* to locate less than one hundredth of a gram of pure radium.

Madame Curie poses in her Paris laboratory.

ALBERT EINSTEIN 1879–1955

Nationality: German-Swiss-American

Profession: Office clerk and mathematician

Biographical information: Einstein was born in Germany and attended college in Zurich, Switzerland. In 1901, he got a job at the Swiss Patent Office, and became a Swiss citizen. In his spare time he worked on difficult mathematical problems. When his work became well known, he returned to Germany. In 1933, he went to the USA and became a US citizen in 1940.

Most famous discovery:
Somewhere among Einstein's work is the simple formula $E=mc^2$. This means that matter (m) can be converted into energy (e), and that the amount of energy will be equal to the amount of matter times the speed of light (c) squared. The speed of light is about 186,282

Albert Einstein

miles per second.. Einstein's formula summarizes what happens when an atom bomb explodes.

Eureka moment: The speed of light was central to Einstein's thinking. One morning, traveling to work by bus, Einstein glanced at the Town Hall clock, if the bus suddenly accelerated to the speed of light, then the clock would appear to stop. The relative motion between observer and observed is at the heart of Einstein's two theories of relativity.

Other discoveries:
Newton's laws of motion do not work mathematically for objects moving very quickly (near the speed of light). Einstein's *special theory of relativity* (1905) extended math to cover objects moving at a constant high speed.

His *general theory of relativity* (1916) further extended math to cover rapidly accelerating objects. As well as showing that matter and energy are interconnected, Einstein also showed that space and time were interconnected, a concept called *spacetime*.

ENRICO FERMI 1901-1954

Nationality: American (born in Italy)

Profession: Physicist

Biographical information: Fermi studied physics at the University of Pisa and was awarded a doctorate for research into X-rays. He worked in Italy until he won the Nobel Prize for physics in 1938. He and his wife then traveled to Sweden and finally to the USA.

Eureka moment: In 1939, Fermi realised that an atom bomb was possible. Together with other scientists, including Albert Einstein, he wrote to US President Franklin D. Roosevelt about the discovery. Roosevelt ordered the Manhattan Project.

Most famous invention: Fermi designed and supervised the

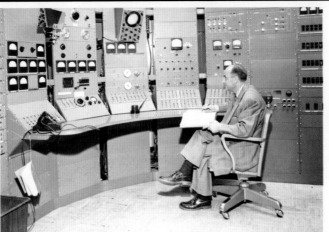

1951, University of Chicago – Fermi at the controls of the new synchro-cyclotron built to study the origins of life.

construction of the world's first nuclear reactor. It was located in a basement squash court at the University of Chicago.

Other inventions: Fermi discovered the first artificial element, neptunium (No. 93) and the element fermium (No.100) is named in his honour.

• See page 11 NUCLEAR POWER for more information on the work of Enrico Fermi.

FRANCIS CRICK & JAMES WATSON

Crick: 1916–2004
Watson: born 1928

Nationality: English (Crick); American (Watson)

Profession: Molecular biologist (Crick); Biochemist (Watson)

Biographical information: Crick studied at Cambridge University and during World War II designed anti-ship mines. Watson trained at the University of Chicago and later studied viruses at the University of Indiana, where he received his doctorate in 1950.

Most famous discovery:
In 1953, while working at the Cavendish Laboratory in Cambridge, Crick and Watson discovered that the three-dimensional structure of the DNA molecule was a double helix.

• See page 15
THE STORY OF DNA

Crick (right) and Watson with their famous laboratory model of the DNA double helix.

Eureka moment: By 1950, scientists knew what DNA was made from, but they had no idea of its shape. Crick and Watson made many models of what they thought it might look like. Finally, they came up with a double helix, shaped like a long, twisted ladder. In 1962, they shared the Nobel Prize for medicine.

A T O Z
INVENTORS

Smith, Richard
Richard Smith, a blacksmith, carpenter, and farmer, encountered the problem of hard-to-remove tree stumps when turning forests into fields in South Australia. The stumps slowed the plowing and broke plows. While plowing one day in 1876, Smith observed that a plow-blade that had come loose rode over a stump and continued plowing. Smith designed and manufactured the flexible *Stump-jump* plow that had blades that were forced back into the soil by weight, after jumping.

Watson-Watt, Robert Alexander
In 1935, Scottish physicist Robert Alexander Watson-Watt was working on aircraft radio-location. He beamed radio waves at planes and then calculated the time it took to receive reflections back. Elapsed time gave him the aircraft's distance away. By late 1935, Watson-Watt was able to locate aircraft 68 milrd away. His work led to the development of the first radar system.

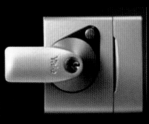

Yale, Linus
In 1861, Linus Yale Jr. perfected the lock with a compact, revolving barrel and flat key that we use today. It was based on a lock designed by his father using a principle known to the ancient Egyptians.

INVENTIONS

Some inventions are the result of years of dedicated research. Others come as a flash of inspiration. An invention may solve a specific problem, or be the by-product of an inventor's irresistible urge to understand how things work and then improve on them. All inventions draw on the accumulation of human knowledge and the work of earlier inventors. Many inventions may not have made the headlines, but they represent the work of inventive men and women around the world.

WORDS OF WISDOM

"To invent, you need a good imagination and a pile of junk."

Thomas Alva Edison

ACUPUNCTURE

This ancient therapy is based on the idea that the life force, or *chi*, flows in certain channels, that can become blocked. The practice of placing a needle in the right place to make the *chi* flow smoothly again has hardly changed since it was first used in China some 4,500 years ago. Steel needles have now replaced stone ones.

ARCHIMEDES SCREW

A means of raising water for irrigation, the Archimedes screw comprises a cylinder with a large screw inside. The bottom of the screw is dipped in water and, as the screw is turned, water is carried up the cylinder. We do not know for sure if Archimedes actually invented this device or whether he wrote about it, but the device came to take his name.

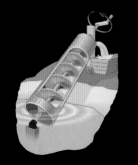

ARCHIMEDES SCREW

ADDER-LISTER

US inventor William Burroughs patented an adding machine that printed its calculations in 1888. With more than 80 keys and a handle to operate the printer, the *Adder-lister* went on sale in 1892.

ADDING MACHINE

The arithmometer, patented in 1820 by Frenchman Thomas de Colmar, was the first calculating machine that really worked. It could add, subtract, multiply, and divide. It took a while to catch on and underwent many developments, but from the mid-1800s onward, hundreds were in use.

AEROSOL CAN

Norwegian Erik Rothheim invented the aerosol can in the late-1920s for packaging paint and polish. Aerosols were developed in the USA for spraying insecticide.

AIR CONDITIONING

In 1902, US engineer Willis Carrier designed an "apparatus for treating air." Carrier's invention was based on cooling the temperature until moisture condenses out, then draining away the water, to produce pleasantly cool, dry air.

AMALGAM FILLING

Before the early 1800s, metal tooth fillings were made by heating metal to boiling point before they were put into the tooth. Around 1826, working independently, August Taveau in France and Thomas Bell in Britain mixed mercury and silver to form a paste, which they found could be inserted cold into the mouth and would harden quickly. The amalgam filling is still used today.

ASPIRIN

In 1899, German chemist Felix Hoffmann re-discovered an old formula for a painkiller. The drug was aspirin, and it contains *salicylic acid*, juice from willow tree bark. Hoffman developed and tested the aspirin and used it to treat his father's arthritis. He patented *Acetyl Salicylic Acid* in 1900.

1899: ASPIRIN

BIKINI

In 1946, the bikini was invented independently by two Frenchmen, Jacques Heim and Louis Reard. Heim designed a very small bathing suit he called the *Atome*, french for *atom*. Reard's creation was named the *Bikini* after the place Bikini Atoll in the Marshall Islands, which was very much in the news at the time due to atom bomb testing taking place there.

1946: BIKINI

BINGO

Originating in Europe, *beano*, as it was first called, arrived in the US in 1929. Toy salesman Edwin Lowe renamed the game *bingo* after he heard someone accidentally call *bingo* instead of *beano*. Lowe hired a math professor, Carl Leffler, to work out combinations for the bingo cards. Leffler eventually created 6,000 different combinations. The game went on to be a popular means of fundraising.

BUBBLE GUM

In 1906, the first bubble gum, called *Blibber Blubber gum*, was invented by Frank Fleer, but the chewy invention never went on sale. In 1928, Walter Diemer, an employee at Fleer's company invents the pink-colored *Double Bubble bubble gum*.

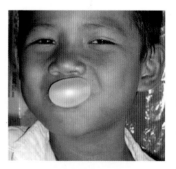

1906: BUBBLE GUM

BUBBLEWRAP

Bubblewrap first appear in 1960 in its earliest form as *AirCap cellular cushioning* and consisted of two layers of soft plastic with bubbles trapped between them. Inventors Alfred Fielding and Marc Chavannes were originally trying to make a textured wall covering.

CAMERA OBSCURA

The modern camera started as a darkened room with a tiny hole in one wall. On the opposite wall, an upside-down image of the outside world would appear. In 1558, Italian physicist Giovanni Battista Della Porta changed the hole for a lens that, by letting in more light, produced a much sharper image. The Italian words *camera obscura* mean *a dark room.*

CAN OPENER

Before 1855, a hammer and chisel were required to open cans. Then, British inventor Robert Yeates invented the can opener—a sharp blade that was stuck in the top of a can, and then worked around.

1855: CAN OPENER

CASH REGISTER

Restaurant owner James Ritty's 1879 cash register displayed the money paid on a dial and recorded it by punching paper on a roll.

CAT'S-EYES

Invented in 1934 by Percy Shaw, the flexible rubber housing enables the reflectors in the center of the road, called *cat's-eyes*, to be cleaned by every car that crosses them.

CHAIN SAW

A ga-engined *sawing machine* was made by German Emil Lerp in 1927. Although similar to a modern saw, it was too heavy for one person to lift. In 1950, the Stihl company produced the first chainsaw light enough for one person.

1927: CHAIN SAW

COMPTOMETER

Displaying its results in a set of windows, US engineer Dorr E. Felt's calculating machine was much faster than its rival, the Burrough's *Adder-lister,* which printed its results. Both machines were in use until the mid-20th century.

COTTON SWABS

This baby cleaning aid was introduced in the USA in 1926. Invented by Leo Gerstenzang after he saw his wife trying to use toothpicks and cotton wool. The sticks were improved in 1958 by a British invention, the paper lollipop stick.

DC06 ROBOT

Manufactured by Dyson in 2005. This robotic vacuum cleaner has sensors to help it avoid stairs and small children. It also remembers where it has cleaned.

DDT

The now little used insecticide *DDT*, a chlorine-based chemical, had been known for years before. In 1939, Swiss chemist Paul Muller discovered that it kills insects, but has little effect on warm-blooded animals.

DIVING SUIT

Augustus Siebe, a German engineer, invented the first practical diving suit in 1819. Siebe's suit comprised of a jacket and an airtight helmet. Air was pumped into the helmet from the surface.

ELECTRON MICROSCOPE

Invented by Ernst Ruska in the 1930s, the electron microscope "sees" with electrons rather than photons of light. Today's electron microscopes make it possible to view items as small as atoms and can display an image on a computer screen.

1930s: ELECTRON MICROSCOPE

ESCALATOR

The escalator can be credited to two inventors in the late 19th century. Inventor George Wheeler sold his idea to a rival inventor, Charles Seeburger, because he had financial problems. Seeburger then sold his patent to the Otis Company and the copyright to the word *escalator,* which he had created for the machine.

• see page 25
OTIS SAFETY ELEVATOR

FERRIS WHEEL

American George W. Ferris designed the first ferris wheel for the 1893 World's Fair in Chicago. Ferris was a bridge builder and owner of a company that tested iron and steel. The finished wheel had a diameter of over 250 feet. Thirty-six wooden cars held up to 60 riders each. The price of a ride was 50 cents.

1893: FERRIS WHEEL

FIELD-ION MICROSCOPE

Invented by Erwin Mueller in 1956, the field-ion microscope has a magnification of more than 2.5 million times.

LAUGHING GAS

Although discovered earlier, in 1799, Humphry Davy found that nitrous oxide could make people laugh. He suggested it might be useful in surgery, but also used it to make party guests laugh (which is extremely dangerous).

LEMONADE

Lemon juice was probably used in drinks for many years before the first commercial lemonade was produced. In 1676, in Paris, vendors, belonging to the *Compagnie de Limonadiers,* sold glasses of a mixture of lemon juice, honey, and water. They poured the lemonade from tanks strapped to their backs.

LETTERBOX

On October 4, 1892, American George Becket patents a house-door letterbox with a self-closing door, now called a *mailbox*. U.S patent number 483,525.

LIE DETECTOR

Originally developed by Czech psychologist Max Wertheimer in 1904, the *polygraph*, or lie detector, monitors blood pressure, pulse, and breathing, all of which can change when people lie.

INVENTIONS

LIQUID PAPER

American secretary Bette Nesmith Graham invented liquid paper by mixing some of her artists' materials in her kitchen blender. When other secretaries noticed Bette using her invention to hide typing errors, they wanted some, too. Bette started her *mistake out* company in 1956.

M&M's

Invented by snack food genius Frank Mars, of Mars bar fame, in the 1930s. Frank wanted to invent a chocolate that had a protective candy coat to stop it melting.

1930s: M&Ms

MACADAMIZED ROAD

In 1783, returning to his native Scotland after making his fortune in America, John McAdam took an interest in the poor state of the roads. He experimented with road surfaces and by 1815, using a mixture of different sized stones, he had perfected a waterproof, durable surface suitable for the coach traffic of the day.

MARGARINE

In 1869, French chemist Hippolyte Mege-Mouries invented a butter substitute, called *margarine*, by bubbling hydrogen through a mixture of vegetable oils.

MATCH

As knowledge of chemicals increased in the early 1800s, inventors used their knowledge to try to create an improved means of light. In 1827, British chemist John Walker produced his *Friction Lights* that lit up when rubbed on sandpaper.

MINER'S SAFETY LAMP

In the early 1800s, many lives were lost due to explosions in mines. The explosions were caused by the flames from miners' lights making the methane gas underground explode. Mine owners commissioned three men to try to find a solution: chemist Humphry Davy, William Clanny, a doctor, and mechanic George Stephenson. The mine owners were pleased with Davy's design, but the miners preferred the lamp designed by Stephenson, who was "one of their own." Eventually most miners' lamps incorporated ideas from all three inventors.

NEON SIGN

Inventors had discovered that low pressure gas in a tube could be lit up with electricity. In 1910, French physicist Georges Claude found that the gas neon produced an intense orange-red glow—not suitable for regular lighting, but great for advertising signs!

1910: NEON SIGN

NITROGLYCERINE

Discovered in 1846 by Italian chemist Ascanio Sobrero, nitroglycerine was the first "high explosive." It was much more powerful than gunpowder. Just dropping a container of the chemical on the floor can cause a large explosion.

OFRO ROBOT

Built by Robowatch Technologies, Germany, *OFRO* robots are designed to carry out surveillance in high security places, such as airports, nuclear power plants, and prisons. *OFRO* is dispatched to respond to alarms.

OIL PAINTING

Oil paint had been known since Roman times, but until the early-15th century, artists used paints made with eggs, such as tempera. The French and Flemish painters Robert Campin and Jan van Eyck perfected the use of oil paints in the 15th century. The graded tones that could be achieved with oil paints gave a greater sense of realism to their work.

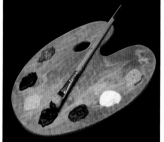

15th CENTURY: OIL PAINTING

OSCILLOSCOPE

A device that makes it possible to see electrical signals on a screen. The cathode ray oscilloscope was invented in 1897 by German physicist Ferdinand Braun.

PACKAGE VACATION

The first "package" vacation was a train trip from Leicester to Loughborough in 1841. The excursion was a success, proving there was a demand for such a service. By 1855, the organizer, British missionary Thomas Cook was organizing trips to Europe.

PAPER CUP

In 1908, US inventor Hugh Moore designed a vending machine to deliver water in individual paper cups. Previously, thirsty consumers had to share a tin cup. Moore's paper cups became known as *Dixies* after the company created to make them in 1919.

PARACHUTE

Frenchman Louis Lenormand gave his invention its first serious trial in December 1783 by jumping from the Montpelier observatory with a 14-foot chute. He landed safely. Although originally invented as a way to escape a burning building, a parachute was used in 1797 by another Frenchman to jump to safety when his hot-air balloon burst over Paris.

PARKING METER

Carlton Magee's invention first appeared in Oklahoma City in 1935. Magee hoped his *Park-O-Meter* would stop all-day parkers taking up spaces on the streets and make a little money for the city.

PENCIL

Having already identified graphite as a distinct mineral in 1565, Conrad Gesner, a German-Swiss naturalist, had the idea of placing the carbon in a wooden holder to form a writing instrument. Modern pencils with a core of graphite glued inside a thin tube of wood were first made in 1812.

1812: PENCIL

PEPSI-COLA®

In 1893, Caleb Bradham a pharmacist in New Bern, North Carolina, began experimenting with soft drink mixtures. Bradham's mixtures were sampled by customers at his drugstore fountain. In 1898, one of his formulations, known as *Brad's Drink*, proved popular and on August 28, it was renamed *Pepsi-Cola*.

In 1902, the trademark was registered and the Pepsi-Cola Company was formed. In 1908, Pepsi was one of the first companies to modernize delivery from horse-drawn carts to motor vehicles.

1893: PEPSI COLA

PLASTERS

In 1920, Earle Dickson, who worked for Johnson and Johnson, invented *plasters*. He stuck together adhesive tape, gauze, and fabric, and then rolled up the plasters for future use. Dickson's invention was soon on sale in the US as *Band-Aid*.

PICK-PROOF LOCK

In 1784, British engineer Joseph Bramah offered £210 to anyone who could pick the lock he had invented. It was 67 years before the reward was claimed by US locksmith A.C. Hobbs, who took 51 hours to pick the lock.

POST-IT NOTE

US company 3M's Post-it notes were launched in 1980. A company chemist, Spencer Silver, made a "not very sticky" adhesive, but it was his colleague Art Fry who suggested the use for it.

RAWLPLUG

Since 1919, when British builder John Rawlings devised his "plug," there has been no need to damage walls when hanging things on them. Rawlings' invention lets you simply drill a hole and then insert a fiber rawlplug that expands to hold the screw.

RING-PULL CAN

The first drink cans required a separate opener. In 1965, US engineer Ermal Fraze patented the convenient ring-pull can. The sharp-edged ring-pulls could be dangerous if thrown away, so engineer Daniel Cudzik invented the "stay-on tab".

ROBART III ROBOT

First made in 1992, *Robart III* is used by the US Navy. It has a camera, infrared sensor, and a gun that can fire darts. *Robart III* was built by Bart Everett of the Naval Oceans Systems Center.

RUBBER

French scientist Charles-Marie de la Condamine discovered rubber trees with their sticky sap while on an expedition to South America. Although other Europeans had come across the substance in their travels, it was Condamine's samples sent back to France in 1736 that put the product on the scientific map. Rubber was named when British chemist Joseph Priestley found that it would rub out pencil markings.

RUBBER BAND

In 1845, Stephen Perry of Messrs. Perry and Co. of London, England, a rubber manufacturing company, invented the rubber band. He used it to hold papers and envelopes together.

SAFETY PIN

US mechanic Walter Hunt invented the modern safety pin in 1849. His design was actually very similar to one that was invented and worn by people 2000 years ago. The clothing clasps were called *fibulas*, and they were used by the ancient Greeks and Romans for fastening clothing.

1849: SAFETY PIN

SCANNING TUNNELING MICROSCOPE

Invented in Switzerland in 1981 by Gerd Binnig and Heinrich Rohrer, the scanning tunneling microscope can be used to study and photograph individual atoms.

SCISSORS

The scissor principle was known in 3000 BC, but scissors like we use today, with two blades that pivot at the center, were invented by the Romans in about AD 100.

3000 BC: SCISSORS

SHOPS

Ancient Greek historian Herodotus (c 480–420 BC) stated, "the people who invented coins also invented shops." He may well have been referring to the Lydians, an ancient civilization from an area that is now Turkey. The first shops were probably trading around 600 BC.

SLICED BREAD

Inventor Otto Frederick Rohwedder began work on a bread slicer in 1912. In 1928, he finally invented a machine that could slice bread and then wrap it to stop it going stale.

SLINKY

In 1943, engineer Richard James invented the Slinky after he witnessed a long coil of metal, part of a Navy experiment, fall from a desk and appear to walk. He took the idea home to his wife Betty, who named the toy *Slinky* after consulting her dictionary to find a word that described the spring's movement. Richard and Betty had just 400 springs made by a local machine shop initally. They soon needed to replenish their stock, when the Slinky was a huge success!

SPECTACLES

The glass workers of Murano in Venice, Italy, invented the spectacles around AD 1275.

AD 1275: SPECTACLES

STEREOSCOPE

By combining two slightly different pictures, one for each eye, a three dimensional image is produced by a stereoscope. Invented before photography by Charles Wheatstone, stereoscopy became a craze after David Brewster showed a version of the stereoscope at the Great Exhibition in 1851.

STICKY TAPE

US engineer Richard Drew first invented masking tape, a sticky paper tape. Then in 1925, by coating cellophane with a similar adhesive, he produced what is known as *Scotch Tape*.

SUPER GLUE

In 1951, US researchers Harry Coover and Fred Joyner realized the potential of the chemical cyanoacrylate, discovered in 1942, for use in a super strong glue. A trace of water is all that is needed to trigger a chemical reaction that turns the liquid glue into plastic.

INVENTIONS

SUPERMARKET

In 1916, in order to cut costs in his business, US grocer Clarence Saunders invented "self-service" at his Piggly Wiggly store in Memphis, Tennessee. It was cheaper to let people take goods from the shelves than have staff members serve them. Saunders had invented the modern supermarket.

1916: SUPERMARKET

SUPERMARKET CART

US retailer Sylvan Goldman noticed that customers at his Humpty Dumpty supermarkets never purchased more than they could carry. In 1937, he had wheels and baskets welded to folding chairs. The supermarket cart was created.

SURGICAL GLOVES

Convinced that germs were a threat to their patients, 19th century surgeons needed to find a way to keep their hands sterile while operating. In 1890, US surgeon William Halsted invented thin rubber surgical gloves, and the problem was solved.

THERMOS FLASK

Based on James Dewar's vacuum bottle, Rheinhold Burger's metal-cased flask was launched in 1904. The name *Thermos flask* was chosen after a competition.

TOOTHPASTE IN A TUBE

Crème Dentifrice, produced in 1892 by US dentist Washington Sheffield, was the first toothpaste to come in a tube. Before Sheffield's innovation, toothpaste had come in a jar.

TRAFFIC SIGNAL

An early form of traffic lights appeared in London in 1868. In 1923, a system using three moving arms was patented in the US by inventor Garrett Morgan.

TRAMPOLINE

Circus acrobat and Olympic medalist George Nissen invented the trampoline in 1936. He built a prototype in his garage and later patented the idea.

TRIVIAL PURSUIT

Described as "a party in a box" and a "revolt against television," the quiz game *Trivial Pursuit* was created by four Canadian friends in 1979. After a slow start, the marketing took off when the game was launched in the USA. In 1984 alone, more than 20 million games were sold.

TYPEWRITER

American mechanical engineer Christopher Sholes patented the first practical typewriter in 1868. Sholes laid the keyboard out in the pattern, known as QWERTY, after the six letters that appear top left on the keyboard. This layout was designed to slow down the typist in order to stop the keys jamming. Modern keyboards still have the same layout.

UMBRELLA

The steel-ribbed umbrella that we use today was invented in England in 1852 by Samuel Fox.

1852: UMBRELLA

VACUUM CLEANER

In 1901, British engineer and inventor Hubert Cecil Booth invented the vacuum cleaner. Booth's large, horse-drawn machine went from house to house sucking out the dirt through hoses. Booth formed the British Vacuum Cleaner Co. in 1903, and built his first canister-style machine in 1904.

1979: TRIVIAL PURSUIT

VELCRO

Patented in the 1950s, Swiss inventor George de Mestral's invention of Velcro came to him after tiny plant burrs (seed pods) attached themselves to his clothes and his dog while hiking in the countryside. Under the microscope, the burrs were discovered to have tiny hooks that were hooked in the fabric of Mestral's pants. Mestral's idea was to produce a two-sided fastener with hooks on one side and soft loops on the other. The name *Velcro* is a combination of two French words, *velours* (velvet) and *crochet* (hook).

VELOCIPEDE

The *draisienne* invented by Baron Karl von Drais de Sauerbrun in 1817 is recognized as the first two-wheeled, rider-propelled machine. Although von Drais called his device a *Laufmaschine* (running machine), *draisienne* and *velocipede* became more popular names. Made of wood, the machine was propelled by the seated rider paddling his feet on the ground. Copies were soon being made in other countries and, in 1818, Denis Johnson of London patented a *pedestrian curricle,* an improved version of a draisienne that he had purchased.

VENDING MACHINE

Drop in a coin and the machine will release a shot of holy water. Ancient Greek inventor, Hero of Alexandria, described this early type of vending machine in a book around AD 60. It is not known if the machine was ever built.

WINDSURFER

Norman Darby's passion for boatbuilding led to his invention of the sailboard or windsurfer. One day in 1943, while out sailing, Norman wanted to cross a stretch of very shallow water. First, he removed the keel of his small boat and then the rudder. He found that he could steer by tilting the sail. From that moment, he worked to perfect a purpose-built board.

ZODIAC SIGNS

The Mesopotamians were very eager star-gazers. Around 500 BC, Astronomer-priests divided the night sky into 12 equal parts and identified each part by a different star constellation. The constellations they recognized are the basis of modern-day star signs and horoscopes.

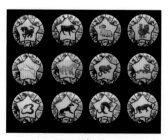

500 BC: ZODIAC SIGNS

WHAT IS A PATENT?

To prevent other people from making, using, or selling an invention without the inventor's permission, he or she must apply to a government patent office to take out a patent.

- If no one else has patented the same invention, a patent will be granted for a specific period of time. Patents usually cover the way things work, what they do, how they are made, and what they are made of.

- Today, most patents are granted to cover newly invented improvements to existing technology.

SOME FAMOUS PATENTS

- **Telegraph**
  US Patent No. 1,647
  June 20, 1840
  Samuel Morse

- **Sewing machine**
  US Patent No. 13,661
  October 9, 1855
  Isaac Singer

- **Electric light**
  US Patent No. 223,898
  January 27, 1880
  Thomas Edison

- **Automobile**
  US Patent No. 686,046
  November 5, 1901
  Henry Ford

- **Airplane**
  US Patent No. 821,393
  May 22, 1906
  O. & W. Wright

- **Packaged frozen food**
  US Patent No. 1,773,079
  August 12, 1930
  Clarence Birdseye

You can see the actual patents of these inventions and others at www.uspto.gov

PATENT PROBLEMS

In theory, it should be very simple to patent your idea. However, in practice, it can sometimes be a long and expensive process if people try to steal your idea, or claim they had it before you.

- Alexander Graham Bell filed his patent application for the telephone on March 7, 1876, only hours before his rival Elisha Gray.

- Gray pursued Bell with 600 lawsuits claiming the idea.

CONCRETE FURNITURE

In 1911, Thomas Edison proposed a new range of home furnishings made from concrete.

- Easy to manufacture and low in cost, Edison's special lightweight concrete would be used to produce phonograph cabinets, pianos, and even bedroom furniture.

- Unfortunately, when Edison shipped some phonograph cabinets to a trade show they arrived in pieces. Not good publicity for a product marketed as being able to withstand being dropped and abused.

- The world was not ready for Edison's new idea, and concrete furniture faded into history.

IT SEEMED LIKE A GOOD IDEA AT THE TIME...

Sometimes inventors are convinced that they have actually found the best thing since Otto Rohwedder's sliced bread—it's just that nobody else appreciates their genius!

Here are a selection of inventions that, for some reason, did not make it into production.

AIR-COOLED ROCKING CHAIR

On July 6, 1869, US Patent No. 92,379 was issued to Charles Singer for his innovative, breezy rocking chair. The chair was to have bellows (devices that were once used for blowing air on fires) connected to a hose that blew air onto the sitter as he or she rocked.

THE VELO-DOUCHE

In 1897, an English bicycle manufacturer contemplated the idea of a *Vélo-douche shower bath*—an exercise bike combined with a shower to keep the rider in shape and clean.

A CUTE INVENTION

On May 19, 1896, US Patent No. 560,351 was issued to inventor Martin Goetze for his device for producing and maintaining dimples on human skin.

SNOW TO AUSTRALIA

Around 1970, an intriguing idea was patented in the UK by inventor A.P. Pedrick. The idea was to irrigate the Australian desert by using the force from the spin of the Earth to pipe snow and ice balls from Antarctica.

CHEWING GUM LOCKET

On January 1, 1889, US Patent No. 395,515 was issued to Christopher W. Robertson for his invaluable invention, the chewing gum locket. Conveniently stashed away in the locket, chewed gum could be safely carried on the person. Far better than leaving it around to get dirty.

BLAST OFF!

In 1500, Chinese scientist Wan Hu tried to fly by tying 47 rockets to his sedan chair. The rockets exploded, and he was never seen again.

WORDS OF WISDOM

"Results! Why man, I have gotten a lot of results. I know several thousand things that won't work."

Thomas Alva Edison

GLOSSARY

AIDS (Autoimmune Deficiency Syndrome) A fatal disease caused by HIV that renders victims susceptible to infections and cancers. AIDS can be slowed, but not cured, by expensive drugs.

Alternating current The flow of electricity supplied to homes and offices through electrical mains. It reverses direction about 50 or 60 times per second.

Anatomist Medical scientist who studies the bones, organs, and other structures that make up an animal body.

Anthropologist A scientist who studies the traditional human societies and cultures that still exist in the modern world.

Archaeologist A scientist who seeks out and studies non-written evidence of past human cultures and civilizations.

Atom Smallest possible unit of a chemically pure element. All materials and substances are composed of atoms and combinations of atoms known as *molecules.*

Atom bomb Device that uses a chain reaction of uranium or plutonium to produce an extremely powerful explosion. A single atom bomb is equivalent to a million tons of ordinary explosive.

Atomic size The atomic size of an element depends on the number of protons and neutrons in the nucleus. An atom of hydrogen has just one proton in the nucleus. An atom of uranium has 92

protons and even more neutrons.

Australopithecus (Southern ape) One of a group of bipedal (using two legs) primates that lived in Africa about 4 million years ago and may have been the ancestors of modern human beings.

Base pairs The four nucleotide bases—thymine (T), guanine (G), cytosine (C), and adenine (A)—that make up the genetic code. They are always arranged in pairs.

Biochemist A scientist who studies the substances produced by living things and how they combine and react with other substances.

BASIC (Beginners All-purpose Symbolic Instruction Code) A computer language that is used to write operating program for a computer.

Bacteria Group of single-celled organisms that are similar to the earliest forms of life. Bacteria do not have a nucleus and do not use DNA. Some bacteria cause diseases.

Binary Using just two digits, 1 and 0. Computers operate according to instructions written in binary numbers. Text and other information (such as sound and video) can be digitized (converted into binary numbers) for storage or transmission.

Botanist A scientist who studies plants.

Calculus A type of arithmetic used to find the solution to problems where there are two variable quantities, as in the complex motion of a cannonball through the air or a planet through space.

Cathode ray tube A hollow glass device that "fires" a stream of electrons from one end so that they form an image on the flattened surface of the other end. The cathode ray tube is the basis for ordinary TV sets.

Census A count of the total population of a country. Many governments conduct a census every ten years.

Centrifugal force The force that appears to make objects on a rotating body move toward the outer edge.

Clone A plant or animal produced from a single cell that is an absolutely identical copy of the plant or animal from which the cell was taken. A clone has exactly the same DNA as the "parent."

Coaxial cable Electrical communications cable with an insulated central strand of thick metal wire surrounded by a woven mesh of fine wires.

Current The flow of electricity around a circuit.

Cyclotron A device used to accelerate subatomic particles (such as protons, neutrons, or electrons) so that they crash into each other to produce other subatomic particles.

Dialysis medical technique for removing harmful chemicals from the blood of patients with kidney failure.

Digital Stored or transmitted in digital form as a series of binary numbers.

Direct current (DC) Electricity, produced by batteries and dynamos, that flows in one direction from a positive anode to a negative cathode.

DNA (Deoxyribonucleic acid) The substance that contains the genetic code used to pass on characteristics to offspring. All living things, except bacteria, use DNA, and every species has its own type of DNA molecule.

Electromagnet A device that only exhibits magnetism when an electrical current is applied to it.

Electron Subatomic particle with a negative electrical charge. Electrons orbit around the nucleus of atoms. Atoms usually have the same number of electrons as protons in their nucleus.

Electron shell The orbit of electrons around an atomic nucleus forms a series of hollow, spherical shells," one inside the other, with the nucleus at the center.

Element One of the pure chemical substances. There are 92 naturally occurring elements, and about 20 short-lived artificial elements that have been made in laboratories.

ESA (European Space Agency) A multinational organization concerned with space exploration and research.

Exposure time Length of time a camera shutter remains open in order to produce an image of the desired quality.

Fiberoptic cable Communications cable made from woven strands of glass, designed to carry messages as pulses of laser light.

Font A set of the letters of the alphabet and the numerals in matching size and style. Printers use many fonts when producing books and magazines.

Genes The means by which characteristics are inherited through DNA. A gene is a section of the genetic code that contains the instructions for one specific thing, such as making a particular protein.

Genome The complete genetic code for a particular species.

HIV (Human Immunodeficiency Virus) The microscopically small substance that causes AIDS (Autoimmune Deficiency Syndrome). HIV is spread from person to person through the blood.

Homo erectus Early type of human that lived between 1 and 2 million years ago. Some scientists believe that *Homo erectus* was a direct ancestor of modern human beings.

Internet An international network of computers developed in the 1970s. The Internet is now used commercially and can be accessed by all computer users with an addional service.

Jurassic Period in earth's history from 208 to 146 million years ago. During the Jurassic period, dinosaurs lived on land.

Meteorologist A scientist who studies the weather.

Microchip Component of electronic devices, also known as an *integrated circuit* or *silicon chip*. A microchip is a small piece of silicon with thousands of tiny electrical circuits on its surface.

Microprocessor Component of electronic devices. A microprocessor is a self-contained microchip that can perform several electronic tasks at the same time.

Minoans Ancient inhabitants of the island of Crete, who developed the first civilization in Europe around 2500 BC. The Minoan capital was the great palace at Knossos.

Morse Code Sequence of dots and dashes representing letters and numbers invented by Samuel Morse and used to transmit messages by flashes of sunlight on a mirror (heliograph) or along electrical wires (telegraph).

NASA (National Aeronautic and Space Administration) The US government agency responsible for space exploration and research.

Negative In photography, a negative is an intermediate stage produced from exposed film. In a negative image, the colors and tones of the original scene are reversed so that light is dark and dark is light. A bright light is then shone through the negative onto light-sensitive paper to produce a positive image.

Neolithic (New Stone Age) Period of human prehistory when people developed farming and pottery. In Europe and Asia, the Neolithic lasted from around 12,000 to 7,000 years ago.

Neutron A subatomic particle. A component of atomic nuclei that has no electrical charge.

Nuclear reactor A device that uses radioactive material (such as uranium or plutonium) to produce a slow, heat-generating chain reaction. Nuclear reactors are used in atomic power stations.

Nucleotide bases Four chemical substances—thymine (T), guanine (G), cytosine (C), and adenine (A)—that are linked together to form the long strands of the DNA molecule. The genetic code is often said to be a code written in just four letters: *T, G, C,* and *A*.

Nucleus The central part of an atom or cell. In atoms, the nucleus is formed of protons and neutrons. In a cell, the nucleus normally contains DNA.

Oscilloscope Device that uses a cathode ray tube to show electrical signals as glowing lines on a glass screen. Oscilloscopes are used to monitor frequency, wavelength, signal strength, among other things.

Ozone Form of the gas oxygen normally found in the upper levels of Earth's atmosphere where it forms a barrier against ultraviolet radiation.

PALEOLITHIC (Early Stone Age) Period of human prehistory when people made cutting implements and other tools from stone. The Paleolithic lasted from about 2.5 million to 20,000 years ago.

Paleontologist A scientist who studies the fossilized remains of prehistoric animals.

Phoenicians People who lived along the eastern coast of the Mediterranean about 3,000 years ago. They were traders and seafarers and around 800 BC, they founded the city of Carthage in present-day Tunisia.

Photograph Image of reality captured by a light-sensitive medium (for example, photographic film) that can be printed onto a sheet of paper.

Photographic plate Sheet of metal or glass coated with light-sensitive chemicals that was used in cameras before the invention of transparent plastic film.

Physicist Scientist who studies the physical properties of substances, and the way that objects of all sizes are affected by force and energy.

Physiologist Medical scientist who studies the operation and activity of the organs in a healthy body.

Plate tectonics The natural mechanism by which the large plates of solid rock that make up the Earth's outer crust "float" on the semi-solid rock beneath and gradually change their position.

Positive In photography, an image is one in which color tones have the same values as the original scene.

Primeval atom Phrase invented to name the unknown and incredibly small state of the universe immediately preceding the theory of the Big Bang that created the universe around 15 billion years ago.

Protein Proteins, created by the body, that are used to build the structures of cells and tissue.

Proton Subatomic particle, component of atomic nuclei that has a positive electrical charge.

Prototype Trial version of a device intended for manufacture.

Protozoa Single-celled animals living in soil and water that are much more highly developed than bacteria.

Radioactivity Harmful emissions from certain substances, such as radium, uranium, and plutonium, that are said to be radioactive. There are three types of radioactivity: alpha rays, beta rays, and gamma rays, that are composed of sub-atomic particles, such as neutrons, protons, and high-energy photons.

Radiometric dating Method of establishing the age of rocks by measuring the rate at which radioactive substances lose their radioactivity.

Resistance The degree to which a material allows electricity to flow through it without losing energy in the form of heat.

Restriction enzyme Substance used to cut the long-stranded DNA molecule into short strands that each contains just a few genes.

Semiconductor Substance, such as silicon, that conducts electricity in a variable and controllable manner. Semiconductors are widely used to make transistors and microchips.

Shadowgraph Outline or silhouette image produced by blocking light from reaching a photo-reactive surface.

Solar-powered Driven by electricity produced from sunlight.

Speed of light Approximately 186,000 miles per second. Light travels at slightly different speeds through different media, for example a vacuum, air, or water. The speed of light through a vacuum is a constant throughout the universe.

Stereoscopic Providing images that have depth (like those provided by a pair of eyes) as opposed to the flat images produced by cameras with a single lens.

Transistor A transistor is a component of an electronic circuit that depends upon the variable conductivity of a semiconductor. Transistors are very small compared with the triode valves and vacuum tubes that they replaced.

Triode valve Fragile glass and metal device used in radios and other electronic devices before the invention of the transistor.

Ultrasound imaging Medical technique for providing images of the inside of a living body by using reflected sound waves.

Vacuum tube A component of early electronic circuits. A vacuum tube was a hollow glass device containing complex arrangements of bare wires. The air inside the tube was evacuated, leaving a vacuum so that the wires did not burn out when they became hot during use.

White light Sunlight that can be split into the colors of the rainbow by refraction through a glass prism and through raindrops.

INDEX

INDEX